The NOTTINGHAM Cook Book

A celebration of the amazing food & drink on our doorstep
Featuring over 50 stunning recipes

FOREWORD

I've been working in the restaurant business in Nottingham for 22 years, now. I've always loved the region and I'm proud to have a business based here.

My passion has always been to celebrate Nottinghamshire and put the county on the gastronomic map. I want to show that we don't have to be run of the mill or ordinary, we can elevate ourselves and prove that we're as good as the best in the world. That's what's great about a book focussing on Nottinghamshire food.

The idea at my own restaurant was always to celebrate food from the British Isles. We're very lucky that Nottingham has such great produce. For instance, we use Green's Mill for our flour and Cropwell Bishop soft cheese has been on our menu for more than two years.

But, we only use local ingredients because they're good. I'm not going to use someone just because they're local. We've hand-picked all the best produce from this region and we're trying to elevate it to provide a total gastronomic experience. Produce is key and without good produce you can't do good food. Our emphasis is on flavours, not on accolades. Flavour comes first and everything else follows. The seasons completely dictate my own menus. If it's good enough for nature, it's got to be good enough for us.

Being a restaurateur is the best job in the world. It's a vocation where I'm allowed to express myself. Food is my medium. I love good food and I've grown up in a family environment that sits around the table and eats together.

I'm very happy to see the food and restaurant industry in Nottingham doing so well. I go out when I can to see what other places in Nottingham are doing. I get my fish and chips from The Cod's Scallops and it's great to see places like Delilah in the city centre doing so well. And there are some real artisan suppliers out there providing some of the best produce available anywhere in the UK. We use them because they're on our door step, but also because we don't want to miss any opportunity to get great produce on our menu.

THANK You

to the following people for making this book possible:

Anne Davies – BBC East Midlands Today

Carl Froch

Chino Latino

Erin Huckle – Experience Nottinghamshire

Frances Finn – Notts TV & BBC Radio Nottingham

Jilly Pearson – Oasis Breast Cancer Trust

Keith Mincher

Sam & Amy – Gem 106

Sarah Thursfield – Experience Nottinghamshire

Sat Bains

Stuart Broad – Notts & England Cricket

Stuart Pearce – Nottingham Forest FC

Yossi Eliyahoo

World Service

The Nottingham Cook Book
©2014 Meze Publishing. All rights reserved.
First edition printed in 2014 in the UK.
ISBN: 978-0-9928981-5-1

Written by: Oonagh Robinson
Edited by: Phil Turner, Amanda Lester
Photography by: Sam Bowles www.portraitcollective.com
Additional photography: Paul Carroll
Designed by: Paul Cocker, Marc Barker
Cover art: Ian Carrington
Contributors: Rachel Heward, Leah Bradley, Nick Hallam,
Sarah Koriba, Vicky Elwick.
Printed by Bell and Bain Ltd, Glasgow

Published by Meze Publishing
Blind Mice Media Ltd
Unit 1 Beehive Works
Milton Street
Sheffield S3 7WL
www.mezepublishing.co.uk
Tel: 0114 275 7709

SAM BOWLES

When I was young I was an incredibly fussy eater – to the point that I remember pretending I was allergic to pineapple, just because I didn't like it.

But that all changed a few years ago. I began travelling more and trying new flavours. Rather than avoiding the things on the menu I didn't know, I started seeking them out, and that's led to me taking a real pleasure in cooking.

Getting to see top chefs like Sat Bains, Sarah Newman (executive chef at Perkins and escabeche) up-close in the kitchen is a real inspiration – as is the passion shown by the guys at Aubrey's Creperie and the Pudding Pantry.

These days, I guess I have a reputation for producing reasonably decent food at home – it's just usually an hour late. The precision with which the professionals deliver their food is incredible, so the next thing I need to work on is my timing.

OONAGH ROBINSON

I grew up in a council house in Bestwood Park where money was tight, but where we always seemed to have the best quality chicken, lamb and beef come Sunday lunchtime.

Whilst I'm certainly not the world's most competent cook, I still insist on getting my own family together to eat around the table and try new ideas with quality ingredients. And that's why I've so enjoyed writing the Nottingham Cook Book.

As a journalist with more than 25 years experience, I've been truly inspired by the fabulous food and drink businesses I've written about here – and I've been amazed by the wonderful produce available on our doorstep.

I've already had a go at lots of the recipes, and I know that I'll be returning to them time and again. I know lots of Nottingham folk will do the same.

AMANDA LESTER

Growing up with well-done meat by my dad (the cautious scientist) and unlimited Findus crispy pancakes (courtesy of my mum's workplace) meant I probably didn't start out with the most sophisticated palate in life!

However, thanks to cooking sessions with my grandma and sister I developed an interest in food, which grew enormously when my husband and I arrived in Nottingham in 2000. We were blown away by the likes of Hart's and Sonny's and before long, dining out at the rapidly growing number of eateries across the city became our favourite pastime.

It also inspired us to start hosting dinner parties at home, though I confess my husband is usually head chef and I am the amiable host!

As a PR consultant I've been fortunate enough to also work with dozens of superb local restaurants over the years, from larger chains such as YO! Sushi and Turtle Bay to Chino Latino and smaller independents including Iberico, Fire & Ice and Moleface Pub Company.

Producing a book that celebrates all that is unique about Nottingham's food and drink scene whilst also providing you with the tools required to try it at home has been an absolute dream. I cannot wait to get stuck into all the delicious recipes with my family and friends. I hope it brings out the chef and host in you too!

The

CONTENTS

Editorial

The Foreword	2
Credits & Acknowledgements	4
The Publishers – Our Nottingham	4
The Nottingham Food Scene	10
The Directory	220

Guest Recipes

Stuart Broad's – Crispy soft shell crab with creamy curry and pink peppercorn	23
Frances Finn's – Lamb tagine	85
Sam and Amy's – Chocolate brownie cupcakes	153
Carl Froch's – Savai steak and sea bass	167
Stuart Pearce – My mum's corned beef pasta	175
Yossi Eliyahoo's – Thai beef salad	217

Chef Recipes

200 Degrees Coffee

Raising the temperature	24
200 Degrees feta & garlic salad	27

Annie's Burger Shack

I'm just looking for New England	28
Annie's fajita burger	31

Asiana

All the right ingredients	32
Asiana's California roll	35

Aubrey's Traditional Crêperie

Come in and say bonjour	36
Aubrey's Crêpes zesty orange & cardamom sauce with caramelised bananas and mascarpone	39

Blue Monkey Brewery

The small & mighty Blue Monkey	40

Brown Betty's

Real food for real people	42
Brown Betty's chicken and halloumi Joe	45

The Cheese Shop

Say cheese	46
The Cheese Shop's blue Stilton dip	49

Clock House Café

Clock in for tea time	50
Clock House's slow-roasted belly of pork	53
Clock House's raspberry & frangipane tart	55

The Cod's Scallops

Living the bream	56
Cod's Scallops deep-fried hake, chips & mushy peas	59

Colwick Cheese

Nice and cheesy does it	60

Delilah Fine Foods

More than a deli... that's Delilah	62
Griddled halloumi, pomegranate & fregola salad	65
Italian speck with black olive tapenade	65

Edin's

Bohemian rhapsody	66
Edin's harissa baked aubergine	69

escabeche

Mediterranean flourish	70
escabeche's slow-cooked pork fillet, celeriac & apple	73
Ham & cheese croquettes	73

Farndon Boathouse

Down by the river	74
Farndon Boathouse's Thai fish bowl	77

Fire & Ice

A pizza the action	78
Fire & Ice's Mexico pizza	81
Fire & Ice's fabulous cocktail creations	
Bridgford Donkey	83
Peach Julep	83

Fred Hallam Ltd

Quality runs in the family ... 86

Fred Hallam's Brancaster mussels
in Starkey's Bramley juice ... 89

Gonalston Farm Shop

Down on the farm ... 90

Gonalston Farm Shop's cote de boeuf ... 93

Hart's

Straight from the Hart ... 94

Hart's Colwick cheesecake with Italian meringue ... 97

Homemade

It tastes better when it's Homemade ... 98

Jasmin's Cajun chicken quesadillas
with Homemade guacamole ... 103

Jasmin's peanut butter banana
and chocolate chip cake ... 105

Iberico World Tapas

Spanish highs ... 106

Iberico's crispy pork belly
with Bramley apple mustard and morcilla ... 109

JT Beedham

Smoke king ... 110

JT Beedham's pork porkolt ... 113

Kayal

The true taste of India ... 114

Kayal's herb dosa ... 117

The Larder on Goosegate

Larder than life ... 118

The Larder's savoury cheesecake with Colwick
cheese heritage beetroot & cobnuts ... 121

MemSaab

Acclaim, awards and authenticity ... 122

MemSaab's Lahori lamb chops ... 127

The Moleface Pub Company

Digging up a Sunday feast ... 128

Moleface's classic prawn cocktail ... 131

Moleface's English roast beef ... 133

The famous Moleface sticky toffee pudding
with toffee sauce and cornish clotted cream ... 137

Perkins

Smoked to perfection ... 138

Perkins beautiful house salad ... 141

Perkins roast venison haunch
smoked beetroot, kohlrabi purée, fondana potato ... 143

The Pudding Pantry

It's all about what you're pudding in ... 144

The Pudding Pantry's carrot cake doughnuts with
caramelised walnuts, orange syrup and
white chocolate and cardamom ice cream ... 147

The Riverbank

Tales from the Riverbank ... 149

The Riverbank's roast scallops
with artichoke purée, roast pumpkin,
pumpkin seeds and Granny Smith ... 151

Sat Bains with Rooms

Gastronomic delights ... 154

Sat Bains' beef cheek and oysters ... 157

The Sauce Shop

Spice up your life ... 158

The endlessly versatile Sauce Shop collection ... 161

Savai

A taste of the old country ... 162

Savai's penne Pugliese ... 165

Shipstone's Brewery

Brewing up a storm ... 168

Sinatra

Old blue eyes is back ... 170

Sinatra's parma ham wrapped monkfish fillet ... 173

Thaymar Farm Shop

We all scream for ice cream ... 176

Thaymar's chicken in stilton,
apricots and mushrooms ... 179

Thaymar's coconut and raspberry cake
wth raspberry and white chocolate topping ... 181

Thea Caffea

Quintessentially English ... 182

Thea Caffea's Eton mess cake ... 185

Tiffin Tea House

Any time is tiffin time ... 186

Tiffin Tea House butterscotch cake ... 189

Tiffin's very own Welsh rarebit ... 191

Tom Brown's

Back to school ... 192

Tom Brown's Amalfi lemon cheesecake,
cassis sorbet, vanilla meringue and black berries ... 195

The Victoria

A proper pub with proper food ... 196

The Victoria's linguine al fruitti di mare ... 199

The Walton Hotel

Classical Elegance ... 200

Jilly Pearson's leek and stilton dip ... 203

Anne Davies's pea and chorizo risotto ... 205

The Walton Hotel's elderflower posset ... 207

The Welbeck Estate

Made at Welbeck ... 208

Welbeck ale and beef cobbler
with Stichelton scones ... 211

World Service

Service with style ... 212

World Service's poached wild turbot
with oyster mayonnaise, fennel and dashi ... 215

The Nottingham
FOOD SCENE

The food scene in Nottingham is amazing – so let's celebrate it!

There are numerous reasons why Nottingham is famous worldwide: Robin Hood, Torvill & Dean, Brian Clough, Goose Fair, Su Pollard...

But these days, there's another reason people are sitting up and noticing the city and the surrounding county – and that's thanks to our amazing food and drink scene.

Foodie delights of all descriptions await here, in the county which gave the world HP Sauce and Shipstone's bitter.

Did you know we're one of only three places allowed to produce wonderful Stilton cheese? Meanwhile, check out Colwick Cheese, the local treat recently reintroduced to the UK market amidst much jubilation – with none other than Jamie Oliver featuring it on his prime time TV show, Friday Night Feast.

The Bramley apple is another Notts hero product, created in the pretty town of Southwell and still celebrated at the annual Bramley Apple Festival every October.

Meanwhile, the School of Artisan Food, on the historic Welbeck Estate, is teaching the world traditional artisan food methods such as bread baking, cheese making and cider brewing.

Let's face it, Nottinghamshire blummin' loves its nosh.

And this book is an unashamed celebration of our superb independent food and drink scene, from Michelin-starred dining and gastropubs to intimate bistros, farm shops and delis brimming with local produce.

The county has food and drink right at its heart, with Nottingham city centre alone boasting more than 300 pubs, bars, cafés and restaurants – that's more per square mile than any other city in Europe, according to tourism experts Experience Nottinghamshire.

This book is packed with profiles of some of these brilliant venues and recipes for you to try at home. It's a chance to savour the great scene that's been created thanks to the passion and talent of some truly inspiring people.

We've got award-winning venues like Restaurant Sat Bains, Delilah, MemSaab, master butchers J T Beedham, World Service, Hart's, Perkins and The Cod's Scallops fish and chip shop.

Our brilliant café and deli scene is also covered, from established family businesses like Brown Betty's, Savai and The Cheese Shop to exciting newer additions Thea Caffea, the Pudding Pantry, Aubrey's Traditional Creperie, 200 Degrees Coffee and, further afield, The Clock House Café at Upton.

A wonderful range of suppliers and shops also get a showcase here with Oriental food specialists Asiana as well as Fred Hallam's of Beeston, Gonalston Farm Shop and Welbeck Farm Shop just for starters.

If you love your pub grub and brilliant beers, we're also taking a closer look at some excellent venues, including the gastronomically gorgeous Moleface Pub Company and breweries Blue Monkey and Shipstone's.

Of course, we've had a peek around some leading city centre venues, such as the phenomenally successful Annie's Burger Shack, Iberico World Tapas, Sinatra, Kayal and The Larder at Goosegate.

And we've travelled out of town to take in the delights of the Victoria Hotel at Beeston, Fire & Ice, Tiffin Tea House and escabeche at West Bridgford, The Walton and that great trio of superbly restored Trentside eateries the Farndon Boathouse, The Riverbank and Tom Brown's Brasserie.

So come on, me ducks, join us on a culinary journey around Nottinghamshire and take inspiration from some genuinely extraordinary food and drink businesses.

Colston
Bassett

Cow's Milk
Pasteurised VEG
£1.95/100g

Stuart Broad's
CRISPY SOFT SHELL CRAB WITH CREAMY CURRY & PINK PEPPERCORN

Notts and England cricketer Stuart Broad spends up to 300 nights a year away from home, so when he gets a rare chance to cook in his own kitchen, he "likes to make a bit more effort than beans on toast."

"I really enjoy any white fish, especially sea bass," he says. "And if I'm cooking for a group of people, that would often be my go-to dish.

"A slow-cooked lamb shank in red wine and garlic sauce is another favourite as the nights start to draw in and of course, a beef Sunday roast with all the trimmings is the biggest thing I miss when I'm away."

Stuart is also a regular at Chino Latino's on Maid Marian Way, where he's attended sushi classes and held charity events. Here, he's recreated one of the restaurant's most popular dishes – also another of his own personal favourites.

Serves one.

Ingredients

150g soft shell crab

20g potato starch

5g shichimi powder

Pinch of dried pink peppercorns

For the curry sauce

5g mild curry powder

5g turmeric

20ml double cream

10g caster sugar

20ml milk

Oil, for frying

Salt

Method

First, make the curry sauce by cooking the curry powder and turmeric spices in a saucepan.

Add the milk, cream and sugar together and bring to the boil, gradually stirring.

Reduce the sauce by half to thicken. Season with a pinch of salt.

To deep-fry the crab, first dust in the potato starch and shichimi powder. Then deep-fry for 4 minutes at 180°c.

Pour the sauce onto a serving plate, sprinkle with peppercorns, sit the crab on top and serve immediately.

Raising the
TEMPERATURE

200 Degrees Coffee is revealing a host of tricks of the trade at its revolutionary new coffee shop and barista school in Flying Horse Walk.

The concept of grabbing a "quick coffee" could be a thing of the past thanks to the launch of a unique new venture in historic Flying Horse Walk.

200 Degrees Coffee, an artisan firm of coffee roasters sourcing beans from Rainforest Alliance certified farms, has opened its first dedicated café just off Nottingham's Market Square. Their mission is to showcase the true flavours and characteristics of exceptionally freshly roasted coffee.

The brainchild of university pals Rob Darby and Tom Vincent, with the support of Tim Moss, the ground floor of the building is devoted to the 200 Degrees coffee shop, serving a range of specialist coffees, drinks and food.

Meanwhile upstairs, the city's first ever barista school runs dedicated courses and one to one sessions for both the public and trade customers.

This highly unusual learning zone provides professional training to the highest possible level for people working in other coffee shops. But it also gives amateur coffee enthusiasts a thrilling chance to get their hands on commercial machines and learn tips on how to make amazing coffee with even the cheapest home kits.

The idea has already caught on, with numerous enquiries, including bookings for team building events.

Rob and Tom, who met at the University of Nottingham, have more than 20 years experience in the café business behind them. They pride themselves on being one of the few coffee shops who freshly roast all their own coffee, this being done at their Meadow Lane roast house (at 200°c to highlight the inherent flavours and aromas of the beans).

Each roast is meticulously tested to ensure great taste, while hand-crafted methods mean the drink genuinely stands out from the crowd.

With a superb range of food to choose from on the counter – including fresh salads, fruits, breads, sandwiches, quiches and delicious sourdough breakfast muffins – the team hope their vision will cause a mini-revolution in café society.

Wake up and smell the coffee, Nottingham.

200 Degrees Coffee's
FETA & GARLIC SALAD

The very definition of fast food – but with a delicious healthy twist.
Serves four.

Ingredients

200g feta cheese

6 garlic cloves

Handful of capers

2 tablespoons chopped oregano

2 tablespoons chopped basil

Ground black pepper

Extra virgin olive oil to cover

20 sun blushed cherry tomatoes, halved

20 green pitted olives, sliced

Handful of curly parsley, roughly chopped

100g rocket

100g watercress

Sea salt

Method

Dice the feta into small cubes, crush the garlic, then mix these along with the basil and oregano in a bowl.

Add some pepper and just enough olive oil to cover the cheese. Mix again, then place in the fridge for at least 24 hours.

Take all the other ingredients and mix them together in a large bowl, sprinkling with sea salt crystals to serve.

An instant lunchtime winner.

I'm just looking for
NEW ENGLAND

Annie's Burger Shack has brought the incredible tastes and atmosphere of a vintage New England diner to Nottingham – and, oh boy, does Nottingham love it.

When Anmarie Spaziano moved to Nottingham from her native Rhode Island in 1994, she had nothing but a suitcase and a guitar in hand – with dreams of a career in music.

Instead, she moved into the food business – starting out with cookies, which she sold at regional food markets until one of her favourite haunts, The Old Angel, persuaded her to take over their kitchen.

That was in 2009 and Annie spent days coming up with 45 different burger recipes – with brilliant names like the Slayer Burger and the Sid Vicious. The operation eventually moved to another pub, the Navigation, where word started getting around about the amazing grub Annie was doing.

And in January 2014, the story reached its zenith when Annie's Burger Shack opened as a stand-alone venue on Broadway, in the heart of the trendy Lace Market. Within months, this cool hangout became THE place to go for great food and a party atmosphere.

Annie's incredible eye for detail has transformed an empty shell into a visually stunning, bona fide diner straight from 1940s America. Décor is made up of baseball bats, moonshine jars, reclaimed timber and black and white family prints.

The joint is fully booked every night and bookings usually have to be made weeks in advance.

The freshly cooked food is based on the same authentic recipes Annie has known all her life. Choose from great looking favourites such as the Sunday Dinner Burger, the Boston Nibbler and The Elvis, complemented by a range of extras, like chilli, Mexican spiced onions and peanut butter and raspberry jam (with not a faddy brioche bun in sight).

With a brand new downstairs bar area offering wonderful snacks and a top selection of beer as you watch old black and white ball games on specially constructed vintage TVs, expect the cult of Annie in Nottingham to keep on growing.

est burgers in the land!
VISIT US AT WWW.ANNIESBURGERSHACK.COM

Schlitz

ANNIE'S
Burger Shack

Annie's
FAJITA BURGER

This traditional burger recipe is from Annie's home state of Rhode Island, New England – where the classic US diner was first born.

Serves four.

Ingredients

For the burgers

800g fresh minced beef

100g fresh minced pork (optional)

1 large free-range egg

2 tablespoons natural breadcrumbs

1½ tablespoons paprika

1½ teaspoons onion powder

½ teaspoon onion salt

1 teaspoon garlic powder

Pinch of salt

Pinch of sugar

4 seeded burger buns

For the salsa

Fresh coriander

½ cucumber, deseeded and finely diced

1 small head iceberg lettuce, chopped

2 large vine ripened tomatoes, diced

½ fresh lemon

1 small red onion, finely diced

For the fajita topping

1 red pepper, thinly sliced

1 yellow pepper, thinly sliced

1 medium onion, sliced

2 jalapeños, roughly chopped

For the fajita seasoning

2 teaspoons chilli powder

1 teaspoon salt

2 teaspoons paprika

1 teaspoon cornflour

1 teaspoon all seasoning salt

1 teaspoon sugar

½ teaspoon onion powder

¼ teaspoon garlic powder

¼ teaspoon cayenne pepper

¼ teaspoon cumin powder

For the garnish

Sour cream

Guacamole

Pitted black olives

Jalapenos

Method

For the burger patties, hand mix all the burger ingredients together, being careful not to over mix as the patties will become tough.

Separate into four equal balls and place in a bowl, cover with cling film and put in the fridge for later.

To make the salsa, mix the red onion, cucumber, vine tomato squares and a good pinch of roughly chopped coriander in a bowl.

Keep it cold and toss with a squeeze of half a lemon (or lemon juice).

Add black pepper to taste and then place in the fridge.

For the fajita mix, add the oil to a frying pan and fry onions until light brown.

Add in peppers and fry together for a few minutes.

Add fajita seasoning and mix until sticky around the vegetables for another 5-7 minutes.

Add a few tablespoons of water to loosen and mix until fully hot sautéed and blended.

Remove from heat and leave to one side.

To cook your burgers, heat a good non-stick frying pan to medium/high heat.

Place the four burger patties into the hot pan. Do not touch them for at least 5-6 minutes, let the cooking side grill until it seals brown.

With a flat spatula, flip them and allow to brown on the other side for about 3-4 minutes.

Now is the time to gauge how well done you would like your burgers.

Flip again to let juices back in and then flip once more.

Put a slice of cheese on top and reduce the heat straight away to low.

Tip: never squish your burgers with a spatula as you will lose all the flavours you have worked so hard to get right.

To serve, reheat the fajita seasoning mix on low heat before serving and get your buns toasting in the grill.

Make sure you have all your toppings ready or ask your friends to do it themselves from separate bowls at the table.

When your buns are toasted, spread mayonnaise lightly on the bottom bun.

Add lettuce to cover the bottom bun, followed by sliced tomato.

Add your fajita mix (I use about half a cup to get the flavour in the burger).

Add a cool dollop of sour cream, a good pinch of cool fresh salsa, avocado or guacamole, black olives and some coriander leaves to garnish.

You want a nice hot burger and fajita topping with a lightly warm crisp toasted bun, with the coolness of the lettuce tomato, sour cream and salsa giving the right flavour combination.

All the right INGREDIENTS

Family run business Asiana has brought the authentic flavours of the Far East to the UK with its unbeatable range of quality foods.

Nottingham-based Asiana is one of the country's leading importers of Oriental food and beverages, with a pioneering mission to bring unique tastes and great ingredients from around the world to the UK.

Founded in 2003, this family business is so much more than a typical Far Eastern supermarket, stocking a vast product range from China, Thailand, Hong Kong, Vietnam, Malaysia, the Philippines, Taiwan, Korea – and everywhere in between.

Not only does Asiana distribute to supermarkets, restaurants and take-aways, it's also a highly successful website at www.asianaltd.com and has a clutch of superb shops around the Midlands, including two in Nottingham.

The first at Woodborough Road is a massive hypermarket selling everything you could possibly need under one roof – a haven for those in the catering trade.

The second site at Goose Gate in Hockley opened in 2012, and is an express version of the Asiana concept – providing a chic and contemporary shopping experience for city dwellers, students and office workers alike.

The shop specialises in marvellous bubble tea, an East Asian blend of fruit and milk teas with an incredible choice of bespoke flavours on offer. This specialist café was developed with the help of both local universities and features the perfect chill-out area, complete with quirky indoor grass and colourful lighting.

The express site also excels in brilliant sushi kits, developing fabulous recipe cards to go with an unbeatable range of ingredients – also sold extensively through Amazon.

With hundreds of products from rice, noodles and sauces to fresh fruit, vegetables, oils and flours, Asiana has every ingredient you can possibly think of for those who've been inspired to create exotic Oriental dishes following far flung travels, or after reading specialist cook books.

Asiana's CALIFORNIA ROLL

Sushi is the classic Japanese dish, but for some reason it's something few
of us dare to try at home. The time has come to put that right. It's simple,
healthy and absolutely delicious. There are certain things you really need to
remember if you want to create authentic sushi: make sure you use high quality
ingredients as well as authentic Japanese seasonings, and take care to cook
your sushi rice right. Once that's done, have fun creating your own recipes by
mixing and matching flavours and ingredients. Here, we get the rice rolling
with one of the real sushi classics... Serves one.

Ingredients

1 cup of cooked Sumo sushi rice

8 Sumo nori sheets

2 tablespoons sesame seeds

3 tablespoons mayonnaise

½ cup of either fresh or imitation crabmeat, finely cut

1 avocado, peeled and thinly sliced in length

½ cucumber, peeled and thinly sliced into long thin matchsticks

Equipment

Sumo sushi rolling mat

Cling film

Method

Cover the bamboo rolling mat with cling film.

Place the nori sheet on top of the rolling mat. Spread cooked rice evenly on top of the sheet and sprinkle with sesame seeds.

Turn the sushi layer over, so that the seaweed is on top.

Mix the crabmeat and mayonnaise in a small bowl.

Spread the crabmeat mixture evenly down the centre of the nori roll, and top with thinly sliced avocado and cucumber.

With the use of the rolling mat, roll the nori and toppings into a log shape.

With a sharp knife, slice into smaller pieces, according to personal preference.

Serve immediately.

Serving suggestion

You may wish to garnish your roll with salmon roe. Serve with pickled ginger and wasabi paste with a dipping option of sushi soy sauce.

Come in and say BONJOUR

Aubrey's Traditional Crêperie is the bijoux Nottingham haunt with a huge reputation for superb Breton crêpes and galettes.

Talented Meg Hale reckons she must have made thousands of crêpes on her trusty billig since opening Aubrey's Traditional Crêperie in West End Arcade in 2009 – but she still gets excited about every single one.

Trained in the authentic crêpe-producing capital Britanny, Meg's small but perfectly formed venue has a uniquely charming and friendly atmosphere with just a handful of tables (be prepared to share) in a space little bigger than your average living room. Yet, the team are handling up to 120 covers on a busy Saturday.

Named after Meg's beloved cat, the concept of Aubrey's may seem simple – but it's the delicious and intriguing array of savoury and sweet fillings on offer that make this food something truly special. The loyal customer base ranges from pensioners to students.

Meg also stocks a range of cidres (it is of tradition in Britanny to wash your galettes and crêpes down with a bowl of cidre) as well as offering her own unique product range, including salted caramel.

She recently found out that the meaning of the name Aubrey is "small, elf-like kingdom." Quite the most splendid description for this formidable eatery.

Aubrey's Crêpes

ZESTY ORANGE & CARDAMOM SAUCE WITH CARAMELISED BANANAS AND MASCARPONE

This sweet filling is usually made for a specialist crêpe batter to a traditional Breton recipe – but is also suitable for many other types of batters, such as a classic pancake mix.

Makes enough for two fillings.

Ingredients

50g salted butter

2 tablespoons caster sugar

2 large oranges, juiced with some zest

3-5 cardamom pods, shelled and seeds crushed

2 bananas, sliced into medium thick rounds

2 slices of orange

2 dessert spoons of mascarpone

Icing sugar to decorate

Method

Melt the butter in a saucepan. Add the sugar, then the juice and finally the crushed cardamom seeds.

Let the mixture simmer until it begins to caramelise. Do not let it burn.

Add the sliced bananas. If the sauce has reduced a lot, add a touch more orange juice and sugar to match.

Cook the bananas for 3-5 minutes in the sauce without stirring too much.

Place your crêpe or pancake on a warm plate and fold into a half circle.

Add the filling, being careful to leave some sauce in the pan. Fold over to a quarter circle.

Drizzle the remainder of the sauce over the top.

To finish, add a slice of orange and a spoon of mascarpone on top and dust with icing sugar.

Enjoy while hot.

* For those who like a bit of a kick to their crêpe, try adding some flaming Grand Marnier.

The small & mighty
BLUE MONKEY

Blue Monkey is the tiny brewery with big ambitions to produce champion beers that can take on the world.

It's only been going since 2008, but already the craft beers of Blue Monkey Brewery have had ale fans in raptures – winning numerous awards and accolades at festivals throughout the land.

Founded by John Hickling and his uncle Trevor Vickers, this Giltbrook-based business is named in honour of the huge blue flames that once climbed into the night sky at the famous Stanton Ironworks in nearby Ilkeston – dubbed by local folk "the blue monkeys."

Several family members had once worked at this now defunct pipe making factory, which ceased production in 2007. But while the furnaces might be long gone, the blue monkeys are once again lighting up the area in a new and much more interesting way.

With Trevor now in sole charge of this thriving brewery, a host of different beers are being produced, from traditional cask-style ales through to artisan hand-bottled specials and cutting edge hop monsters.

Quirky names like 99 Red Baboons, Guerilla, Bonobo and Ape Ale are amongst the regular selection, or how about seasonal specials such as the Scarlet Chimpernel and Right Turn Clyde?

The Organ Grinder at Canning Circus is the official Blue Monkey pub, while the revamped shop at Giltbrook offers a range of bottled beers including seasonal specials. In addition, you can buy mini casks, gift bags and glassware here.

This year alone, Ape Ale took silver in the strong bitter category at CAMRA's Champion Beer of Britain awards. Meanwhile at Nottingham Beer Festival, Blue Monkey beers won no less than five gold titles.

Capable of brewing up to 18,000 pints of beer a week, Blue Monkey may be small compared to some of the big breweries, but this tight knit team of beer nerds is committed to quality and consistency.

Real food for
REAL PEOPLE

Generations of Nottingham people have enjoyed the tasty homecooked breakfasts and lunches at Brown Betty's, the ultimate family-run "sandwich" shop.

Elizabeth Elliott says food has always been her biggest passion, observing: "The only thing I ever knew was how to cook."

And in 1985, her enthusiasm took on a new life when she established iconic Nottingham eatery Brown Betty's in St James' Street – much more than a mere sandwich shop but an innovative foodie paradise.

The business soon became a real family affair with husband Brian joining Elizabeth, closely followed by sons James and Boyd in the early 1990s.

Elizabeth recalls that The Eighties was a time when words like chilli and samosa were still exotic and strange ideas to Nottingham folk, but the concept gradually grew – and now almost 30 years later the queues out the door each day tell their own story.

Brown Betty's boasts the largest selection of ciabatta and sandwich fillings around. Generations of people have enjoyed the unusual offerings, with customers ranging from the very young to the very old.

Blackboards inside the tiny but quirky shop/diner showcase tempting salads, pasta, ciabattas, curries, rice dishes as well as the house speciality, the Sloppy Joe – full of fiery flavours and mouthwatering character.

It's a real home from home thanks to this close-knit family, with James – a graduate of the catering school at the former Clarendon College – coming up with many of the clever recipes ideas. Meanwhile, Elizabeth still does the washing up and cooks the pasta.

Proud to serve an evolving city and excited to be setting many of the trends when it comes to new ideas, flavours and recipes, Brown Betty's motto is "real food for real people."

And there really is nothing pretentious here, just good food and great service with a smile – even after 30 years.

Brown Betty's

Brown Betty's
CHICKEN & HALLOUMI JOE

This is a fabulous house speciality, based on the original Sloppy Joe favoured in the US and Canada.

Serves four-five.

Ingredients

4 chicken breasts, diced

2 large red onions

2 tins chopped tomatoes

1 tablespoon tomato purée

1 teaspoon dried basil

1 teaspoon dried oregano

4 cloves of garlic, finely sliced

Pinch of salt and coarse pepper

1 jar passata

Water

2 tablespoons olive oil

2 packets of halloumi

Mixed olives

Pickled jalapenos

1 large ciabatta or a selection of smaller ones

Method

Preheat a large pan and add olive oil.

Add the chicken, diced onions, salt and pepper, browning the meat on a medium heat.

Turn the heat down low and add the garlic, stirring constantly.

Add the tomatoes, passata, tomato purée, herbs and an empty tomato tin full of cold water.

Turn the heat high. Stir and bring to a simmer.

Cook for 45 minutes on a low to medium heat, checking to make sure the mixture does not stick to the bottom of the pan (if it does, turn lower and add a litre of water).

Ensure chicken is fully cooked and check the taste of the sauce, seasoning as necessary.

Leave to cool with a lid on.

Fry your halloumi with olive oil, drain and leave to rest.

Toast the ciabatta after slicing in half.

Place bottom half of your ciabatta on a serving plate and spoon over the chicken.

Layer with halloumi and crown with mixed olives and jalapenos. Carefully place on the top half of the ciabbata and serve immediately.

Say CHEESE

The Cheese Shop is the beating heart of a thriving Nottinghamshire food tradition – selling more than 200 British cheeses including famous Stiltons from Colston Bassett and Cropwell Bishop Creameries.

Brothers Webb and Rob Freckingham founded this venerable Nottingham institution in 2004, moving to their current spot in Flying Horse Walk around two years ago.

Former chef Webb teamed up with Rob, who had been carrying on the family farming business, to begin the brave venture at the height of a new era of popularity for British cheeses – previously the poor relation to more glamorous European counterparts.

Whilst the shop and deli café are packed with scrumptious treats from all over the world, the brothers are committed to supporting quality British produce – and particularly the thriving community of East Midlands cheese producers and associated businesses.

"We pride ourselves on knowing our suppliers by name – they are all good friends," Webb enthuses.

Named one of Rick Stein's food heroes in the early 2000s, the Cheese Shop's legendary counter is full of the very best examples of the industry. There's an array of favourites including Royal Basset Blue, Stilton, Stinking Bishop, Smoked Dorset Red, Wensleydale, Camembert and Brie – with new additions to this colourful display virtually every day.

A regular at many of the big outdoor shows in the East Midlands, The Cheese Shop is packed with deli favourites from marmalades and petits fours to biscuits, olives and chutneys.

The friendly café is at the heart of the business, with a new menu every day serving tasty light lunches such as Melba toast with Colwick cheese, cucumber and onion, pig platters, potted shrimps and crumpets and Scotch egg with chutney.

The genial hosts also entertain their regulars with lively banter and jokes – no wonder they're known affectionately as "The Truckle Brothers."

The Cheese Shop's
BLUE STILTON DIP

An easy and quick treat using one of Nottinghamshire's most famous food products.

Ingredients

200g blue Stilton, crumbled

1 garlic clove, crushed

200ml double cream

Juice of half a lemon

25ml white wine

Freshly ground pepper

Method

Combine all the ingredients in a bowl.

Beat well together to form a smooth paste.

Transfer to a small dish and chill well.

Serve with bread sticks, carrot and celery batons.

Clock in for
TEA TIME

Edward Halls has worked alongside Michelin-starred chefs and even cooked at private events for royalty, but now he runs the charming Clock House café and tea room in Upton.

When Edward Halls moved to Nottinghamshire from Suffolk in 2013, he'd already spent many years as a fine dining chef and had also run a successful gastropub, winning numerous awards and accolades.

But having worked exhausting restaurant hours for so long, the Michelin trained chef felt it was time for something a little simpler – and that's when he spotted an opportunity to open a café and tea room at historic Upton Hall, near Southwell.

He approached owners the British Horological Institute and in October last year, the appropriately named Clock House opened, winning an immediate army of eager fans.

Edward has brought a lifetime of fine dining skills – including a spell as a private chef at Kensington Palace – to the fore at this charming venue, which specialises in beautifully cooked breakfasts, brunches, lunches, afternoon teas and amazing Sunday roasts.

With little on the menu board over £10, everything at this eatery is homemade or sourced from a local producer. Still in the kitchen five days a week, Edward focuses on exceptionally good but very simple food with full English breakfasts, superb sandwiches and homemade scones to name but a few favourites.

There are also regular fine dining evenings, where you can enjoy a set menu with six delicious courses, including canapé, appetiser, starter, main, dessert or cheese, tea/coffee and petit fours using the very best local and seasonal ingredients.

Brilliantly, Edward also passes on his vast food knowledge at the popular Clock House cookery demonstration events, aimed at novices and more accomplished cooks alike. Pop along and enjoy your first attempt at bread making or filleting a fish – or maybe find out how to cook the perfect egg custard tart.

Then, enjoy the fruits of your labour and some "time-honoured" Clock House culinary tips. You'll even enjoy complimentary tea and coffee and get notes and recipes to take away.

The Clock House's
SLOW-ROASTED BELLY OF PORK

A slow roasted method gives incredible tenderness and flavour – try a rare breed pork such as Gloucester Old Spot or Oxford Sandy Blacks. Serves eight.

Ingredients

2kg free-range pork belly, boned out, skin removed and crackled separately

2 tablespoons thyme leaves

50g salt

1 teaspoon fennel seeds

3 onions, roughly chopped

3 carrots, roughly chopped

300ml dry cider

300ml good chicken stock

1 tablespoon white wine vinegar

3 sprigs thyme

1 teaspoon peppercorns

4 bay leaves

2 star anise

Method

Lay the pork belly flat and blend the salt, thyme and fennel in a food processor.

Sprinkle this salt mix over both sides of the pork and leave in the fridge overnight, then rinse off excess salt and pat dry.

Roll and tie the pork into a log shape, it's useful if you have someone to help.

Place the chopped onion and carrots into a high sided roasting tray or casserole dish and rest the pork on top.

Place the cider, stock, white wine vinegar, herbs and spices in a saucepan and bring to the boil, then pour gently over the pork. It may not completely cover the pork, but that is fine.

Cover the pork with a piece of baking parchment and then cover the tray with two layers of foil, tucked tightly over the sides so the liquid doesn't escape. Alternatively if you have a tray or casserole with a lid this will work well.

Place in a preheated oven at 100°c for 10-12 hours. It is done when you can push a spoon through the pork with little resistance.

Allow to cool in the liquid, and then remove the pork, cover and refrigerate overnight.

To get perfect crackling, slice the skin into strips and lay on a tray, sprinkle with table salt and roast at 200°c for 10 minutes.

Drain the fat and put back in the oven. Repeat this every 5-10 minutes until it is rendering no more fat and starts to crackle.

When nearly done, turn the oven up to maximum (about 250°c) and check every 2-3 minutes as it puffs up. This will keep in a tub for several days.

Strain the liquid into a pan, skim off the fat and reduce to a sauce.

Slice the pork into portions and fry in a hot pan to colour then in an oven at 200°c, for 8-10 minutes to reheat, add the crackling for the last 2 minutes to crisp.

Serve with buttery mash, crackling, some seasonal vegetables and pour over the sauce.

The Clock House's
RASPBERRY & FRANGIPANE TART

This is amongst The Clock House's most popular sweet treats, served warm
with a little clotted cream. And why not? Serves eight.

Ingredients

For the sweet pastry

125g butter

½ teaspoon salt

70g caster sugar

300g plain flour

1 egg

15g water

For the frangipane

225g ground almonds

225g icing sugar

225g soft unsalted butter

60g plain flour

½ teaspoon salt

4 whole eggs

250g fresh raspberries

Apricot jam to glaze

Method

Make the sweet pastry by rubbing the butter, salt and sugar into the flour until it resembles breadcrumbs.

Add the beaten egg and water and bring together until it forms a dough.

Divide, wrap in cling film and refrigerate for at least 30 minutes.

Line a 23cm tart tin (one with a removable bottom is easiest) with sweet pastry. Roll as thin as possible and ensure there are no cracks.

Rest in the fridge for 15 minutes then place a double layer of cling film in it and fill with uncooked rice. Place in the oven at 160°c for about 20-25 minutes.

Remove and carefully lift out the cling film and rice, holding the edges. Place back in the oven for a further five minutes until the pastry is fully cooked and golden.

Combine all the frangipane ingredients together in a bowl and whisk until thoroughly combined.

Stir in the raspberries, reserving a few to arrange on the top.

Spoon all the mixture into the blind baked pastry case, smooth until even and push the remaining raspberries into the surface.

Bake at 160°c for about 30-40 minutes until there is no wobble and it is deep golden in colour.

At this point, warm some smooth apricot jam in the microwave or in a pan and brush it all over to glaze.

Trim the excess pastry from the sides with a knife and allow to cool for at least 20 minutes.

Living the BREAM

John Molnar has transformed the humble chippy into a gourmet dining experience at the The Cod's Scallops in Wollaton.

This astonishing venue at Bramcote Lane in Wollaton is officially just a fish and chip shop, but with an impressive list of take-away and eat-in choices, it's clear that, here, the concept has been taken to a whole new level.

Offering a wonderful wet fish counter packed with up to 20 varieties such as line-caught cod, haddock, hake, lemon sole, mackerel, and more less known species like gurnard and dab. There is also an impressive range of shellfish on display including lobster, whelks, mussels, oysters, cockles and dressed-crab.

Opened in 2011 by John Molnar, the man behind the hugely successful Moleface Pub Company, the mission at The Cod's Scallops is to showcase the huge variety of delicious fresh fish available in the UK.

You never know quite what will be advertised on the menu boards on any given day, it all depends on what's finest that day. And when it's gone, it's gone, so you need to be an early bird.

The bright and welcoming shop and restaurant has a smashing seaside look, complete with striped décor, high stools and diner-style seating booths. You can also enjoy a glass of prosecco or a pint of beer with your meal.

All the fish here is fried in traditional beef dripping or baked with garlic and lemon. And there are extras, like their own-recipe ketchup, tartar sauce, proper mushy peas and chip shop curry sauce – all served with, or without, batter bits.

There is also plenty for a sweet-tooth such as homemade ice cream, or a range of freshly baked puddings.

The venue has not surprisingly won numerous accolades, including Best Newcomer at the National Fish and Chip Shop Awards 2014 – and even local legend Sat Bains pops in every Monday to get his beloved takeaway.

Fish so fresh, tomorrow's is still in the sea – the witty Cod's Scallops strap line says it all.

The Cod's Scallops
DEEP-FRIED HAKE, CHIPS & MUSHY PEAS

After cod and haddock, hake is The Cod's Scallop's third most popular fish. The majority is landed on the port of Peterhead, Scotland – and the shop only uses 2kg plus fillets giving a chunky, thick portion of fish.
Serves four.

Ingredients

4 x 250g chunks of fresh hake

1.2 kg Agria, Maris Piper or King Edward potatoes.

Beef dripping for frying

200g marrowfat peas

2 teaspoons bicarbonate of soda

Water to cover

Malt vinegar, salt and white pepper to season

2 lemons, halved

Self-raising flour

Baking powder

Salt

To garnish

Tartar sauce

Mayonnaise

Capers

Gherkins

Flat leaf parsley

Lemon

Salt & pepper

Sliced white bread & butter

Method

Try to use beef dripping for frying. This can be pre-ordered from any good butchers, though other fats and oils are fine to use.

For the hake

Get your fishmonger to scale and pin bone your hake portions, but leave the skin on. (Pre-order a larger fillet (2kg+) from your fishmonger, this will give you thick square portions).

For the batter

Mix a few tablespoons of self raising flour with salt, ice cold water and baking powder then whisk until it's the consistency of double cream.

Always keep your batter chilled until you're ready to fry. Give it a quick whisk to check the consistency is still good before use. Store in a stainless steel bowl as this will keep your batter extra-chilled.

When you are ready, dip the fish in the batter and deep fry at 180°c for 7-8 minutes.

For the chips

Our favourite potato for chips is the Agria; because of the taste. Do not use jacket potatoes as this will give you a dark, soggy chip.

Mushy peas

Pre-soak your marrowfat peas for 24 hours making sure you have four times more water to peas as they will swell. Store in a large container to avoid the peas escaping all over your kitchen floor.

Rinse off your peas and put in a saucepan. Cover with water and add bicarbonate of soda Cook on a medium heat until mushy. The peas will need skimming occasionally to remove any scum.

When cooked, season with vinegar, salt and white pepper.

For the garnish

Try tartar sauce, good quality shop-bought mayonnaise, capers, mini-gherkins, flat leaf parsley, lemon zest, salt and pepper. Serve your fish and chips with thickly sliced homemade bread and butter.

Nice and
CHEESY DOES IT

After disappearing for decades, the distinctive Notts speciality Colwick Cheese is back on the market, with a little help from the wonderful Belvoir Ridge Dairy in Eastwell.

The delicious full fat soft cheese was enormously popular throughout the region and was once made in dairies all over Notts, featuring a truly distinctive flavour. But by the early 1990s, it fell out of fashion and, with its short shelf life, demand dwindled.

But now it's back!

Thanks to Belvoir Ridge Dairy at Crossroads Farm in Eastwell, the forgotten delicacy has been revived using traditional methods and milk from rare breed Red Poll cattle.

Owners Alan and Jane Hewson and family have run this Vale of Belvoir farm for three generations. In fact, Alan's favourite job of the day is still milking the award-winning, pasture fed cows – amongst which are many other rare breeds like Blue Albion, Kerry and Dairy Shorthorns.

Alan and Jane are thrilled to be bringing back local lost artisan cheeses – and their new interpretation of Colwick Cheese has had a phenomenal impact.

Colwick Cheese featured on Jamie Oliver's Friday Night Food Feast in January 2014 – an appearance that led to it completely selling out at many shops.

Used in savoury and sweet dishes, the bowl-shaped cheese is still handmade in a cloth. Now lightly salted, it's particularly great cubed and tossed in a salad with a fruit vinegar dressing, or stirred into a risotto just before serving. It's also perfect on pizza or on an antipasti board, with a sweet chilli sauce.

A refrigerated Landrover now brings the fresh cheese to Nottingham's shops and restaurants each Wednesday.

Meanwhile, Open Farm Sunday in June gives people the opportunity to visit this fascinating farm and dairy and learn more about its champion milk, which is sold via a vending machine and is soon to be available in cartons.

More than a deli...
THAT'S DELILAH

Delilah has been a must-do fixture on the food and drink scene in Nottingham since 2005, demonstrating a passion for endlessly interesting produce from around the world.

For a venue that, according to founder Sangita Tryner, really didn't set out to be a café, Delilah certainly oozes that uber cool, laid back vibe beloved of café society.

The imposing and elegant full-height Victorian interior with marvellous floor to ceiling shelving, intricate original features and mezzanine floor is a wonderful setting for a hearty breakfast, morning coffee, imaginative lunch or afternoon platter.

But Sangita sees her hugely popular empire as more of a "deli with tables." Showcasing the vast array of products sold in the shop that has always been the main purpose of this vibrant and exciting business.

Sangita opened the original Delilah on Middle Pavement in 2005, inspired by the superb ingredients and dishes from around the world, discovered during her many years in the food industry.

She quickly managed to fill a gap for Nottingham foodies, moving to the new and much more appropriately spacious spot on Victoria Street in 2012.

With the café side doubling up as an instant tasting forum for everything the deli sells, the emphasis is still on small artisan producers from around the world – including many familiar local names.

"You probably don't come in for a quick ham sandwich," Sangita says. "More likely for genuine New York pastrami on Welbeck sourdough, or frazzled chorizo, alioli and piquillo peppers on real Italian focaccia."

The deli is crammed with produce from every corner of the planet, with the finest cheeses and meats, speciality breads, chutneys, jams, pasta of all shapes and colours, chocolates, cookies, curds and condiments.

Sangita's husband Richard takes care of the impressive wine range, hunting out benchmark wines and unusual grape varieities alike, from small, innovative, quality obsessed and often family-owned producers.

The staff roster has grown from nine to 21 people, under general manager Nik Tooley, who says that "passion for food and commitment to great service" are key qualities looked for when recruiting.

Delilah has become an institution in Nottingham, and beyond, with an array of local and national awards under its belt.

Delilah's Griddled Halloumi
POMEGRANATE & FREGOLA SALAD

Serves four.

Ingredients

300g 'Vallebona' fregola (Sardinian pasta)

250g halloumi, sliced into 12

180g oak roasted tomatoes

1 pomegranate with seeds removed and set aside

1 preserved lemon, sliced into 5mm thick rounds

10g parsley, chopped

10g mint, chopped

10g coriander, chopped

50g wild rocket leaves

For the dressing

40ml extra virgin olive oil

15ml pomegranate molasses

Juice from ½ a lemon

Sea salt

Balsamic vinegar, reduced

Method

Bring a medium pan of salted water to the boil and add the fregola pasta. Boil for approximately 8 minutes until cooked through. Drain, refresh with cold water and set aside to dry.

Meanwhile, place the halloumi slices onto a hot griddle and cook for 2 minutes on each side.

Combine the oak roasted tomatoes, pomegranate seeds, preserved lemon, parsley, coriander and mint in a mixing bowl with the fregola and the dressing.

Place fregola into a bowl. Arrange the griddled halloumi and the rocket over the top with a splash of olive oil and drizzle of balsamic reduction.

Delilah's Italian Speck
WITH BLACK OLIVE TAPENADE

Serves four.

Ingredients

4 slices Welbeck sourdough bread

200g black olive tapenade

120g speck (cured Italian ham)

180g oak roasted tomatoes

200g buffalo mozzarella

40g wild rocket

20ml balsamic glaze

20ml garlic infused olive oil

20ml extra virgin olive oil

Method

Drizzle the garlic oil over the sourdough and toast on a medium/high griddle pan.

Spread olive tapenade over the sourdough and arrange the speck, oak roasted tomatoes and mozzarella on top.

Place the bruschetta under the grill until the cheese has melted.

Arrange 10g of rocket over each bruschetta and drizzle over with extra virgin olive oil and balsamic glaze. Serve immediately.

Bohemian RHAPSODY

Edin's has brought a touch of Bohemian flair to Nottingham with two extraordinarily cool venues in trendy Hockley.

The name Edin's has been around in Nottingham since 1998, with the opening of a vibrant Deli Café in Broad Street.

Specialising in tasty tapas with regular live music in the downstairs bar, it was the brainchild of Sarajevo-born Edin Gondzic, who had switched career from law to food having been inspired by a mum who was an exceptionally good cook.

A second venue, Edin's Kitchen and Patisserie, opened in Carlton Street in 2013, continuing the flamboyant but friendly ambiance in another great location.

The emphasis at each venue is on a relaxed café ambience, with fresh bistro style dishes and a buzzing, continental feel. No wonder both have been recommended by the Cool Places UK website – which picks out the very best places to visit in the country.

Favourite dishes at Edin's Kitchen include spicy lentil stew with halloumi, with a selection of great sandwiches on artisan bread, and mains ranging from butternut squash and cumin seed soup to fresh lobster with lemon butter, sweet potato wedges and dressed leaves. Be sure to try the tasty breakfast menu as well.

There's a mix of authentic styles and influences from a number of different cultures, which all blend together to create unique flavours.

Meanwhile, at the Deli Café, tapas remains a hugely popular choice, with sumptuous fried halloumi, divine courgette fritters and stuffed vine leaves amongst the highlights. Those with a sweet tooth particularly clamour for the baklava – the legendary treat which, according to the Edin's team, is sold here by the tray full.

Edin himself still goes to the best food markets to source the finest quality ingredients around, and he's still a big part of the home from home, rustic atmosphere created at both venues.

Photo: Gaelle Citharel

Photo: Gaelle Citharel

Edin's Harissa
BAKED AUBERGINE

An excellent lunch or supper dish from the Middle East,
ideal for vegetarians. Serves two.

Ingredients

For the harissa

1 red pepper

½ teaspoon coriander seeds

½ teaspoon cumin seeds

½ teaspoon caraway seeds

½ tablespoon olive oil

1 small red onion, roughly chopped

3 cloves garlic, roughly chopped

3 hot red chillies, deseeded and
roughly chopped

½ tablespoon tomato paste

2 tablespoons lemon juice

½ teaspoon salt

For the saffron yoghurt

500ml natural yoghurt

1½ tablespoons runny honey

5-8 strands of saffron

For the aubergine

2 medium aubergines (150-200g)

1 tablespoon salt

2 tablespoon olive oil

To garnish

Cumin seeds

Flaked almonds

Pomegranate seeds

Seasonal leaves

Method

For the harissa

Place the pepper under very hot grill until blackened all over and soft.

Transfer to a bowl and cover with cling film. Leave to cool; this will allow for the skin to almost steam away from the flesh making it much easier to peel. Peel and deseed.

In a hot, dry pan toast the seeds for 2-3 minutes until aromatic. Grind into a powder.

Heat the olive oil and fry the onion, chillies and garlic until dark and smokey for 10-12 minutes, until almost caramelised.

Combine all elements into a food processor and liquidise. Add a little more oil if necessary.

If stored in a sterilised jar, this should keep in the fridge for 2-3 weeks.

For the saffron yoghurt

Incorporate ingredients together and mix well every hour or so to bring out a strong yellow colour. For best results, prepare the day before.

For the aubergine

Cut the aubergines lengthways and score in a crisscross pattern ensuring you do not pierce the skin.

Season the flesh generously and rub the harissa paste all over the aubergine making sure to incorporate it within the scores that you have made.

Place onto a baking tray, drizzle with good olive oil and bake in a fan assisted oven for 25-30 minutes at 180-200°c.

To assemble the dish, spread a thin layer of harissa around the edge of the plate. Place aubergine on the plate in the centre and drizzle with saffron yoghurt. Garnish plate with toasted cumin seeds, flaked almonds and pomegranate seeds. Top the aubergine with cous-cous and finally dress with some tossed seasonal leaves (preferably rocket, lambs lettuce or watercress).

Mediterranean FLOURISH

Uno, dos, tres, eat – escabeche has brought the fresh taste and relaxed mindset of Spanish dining to the heart of West Bridgford.

You might be forgiven for thinking you'd walked into one of the cool eateries of Barcelona's Old Town when you first step inside escabeche.

This chic tapas bar and restaurant in the centre of a booming West Bridgford takes culinary, atmospheric and visual inspiration from the Spanish capital – offering a wealth of choice seven days a week.

Here is a place where fresh, quality ingredients and dishes provide superb value in a relaxed, contemporary setting. escabeche prides itself on being a venue where friends and family can relax and share great food, drink and a welcoming ambience.

Opened in 2010 by Nottinghamshire's renowned Perkins Family, escabeche serves delicious, freshly cooked tapas, raciones, stone baked flatbreads and a host of other authentic delights. Amongst the highlights are brilliant breakfasts, their amazing value menu del dia and a host of ever changing fresh specials.

Only the best quality produce makes the grade and the team source ingredients both locally and from further afield, with many specially imported items for that genuine Mediterranean flourish.

The innovative drinks offering is equally hand-picked – think cool cocktails and sangrias, beautiful gin tonics, craft beers and ciders including escabeche's own labelled organic lagers, interesting wines and sparklers with a distinct Spanish focus, alongside refreshing smoothies and shakes.

Casual and laid-back by day, escabeche bursts into life when the sun goes down. Meanwhile, the popular escabeche Sunday roasts give this classic staple a Mediterranean twist; all rounded off later in the day by live acoustic music sessions providing yet another highly original offering for those winding down following a busy weekend.

What remains constant throughout at escabeche is the deep commitment to exciting food, informed service and great quality.

Salud, West Bridgford!

escabeche's
SLOW-COOKED PORK FILLET, CELERIAC & APPLE

These authentic and great looking dishes are perfect for sharing. Serves four.

Ingredients

400g pork fillet

1 large head celeriac, peeled

1 orange

1 lemon

1 apple

2 cloves garlic

Sprigs of thyme

Sprigs of rosemary

3 tablespoons olive oil

250ml milk

100ml double cream

Butter

Sea salt

Method

Trim the pork fillet to remove any sinew and cut into four equal portions.

Zest the orange and lemon, crush the garlic and finely chop some thyme and rosemary.

Rub well onto the pork fillets along with half a teaspoon of sea salt and the olive oil. Cover and marinate overnight in the fridge.

Make the purée by cutting half the celeriac into 3cm chunks. Place in a pan with the milk, double cream and half a teaspoon of salt plus a few sprigs of thyme.

Cook gently on the hob until the celeriac is tender.

Separate the celeriac from the cooking liquid and blitz in a blender until smooth, adding enough liquor to reach the desired consistency.

Cut the remaining half of the celeriac into 1cm cubes. Put equal parts butter and water into a pan. Add celeriac and simmer until al dente.

If using a water bath, cook the pork in a vacuum packed bag at 60°c for 40 minutes.

Alternatively, tightly roll the portions into individual 'sausages' using cling film. Preheat a tray of water in the oven to 60°c and cook the pork for 40 minutes, ensuring all the meat is submerged.

To serve, heat the celeriac purée. Remove the pork from the bag/cling film and sear all sides in a hot frying pan.

In the same pan, colour the cubes of celeriac on all sides and finish with butter.

Slice the pork into three pieces and drain any excess juice onto a clean towel.

Serve on top of the celeriac purée and scatter the celeriac cubes. Season the sliced pork with a little sea salt if required. Slice the apple into thick batons to finish.

HAM & CHEESE CROQUETTES

For the ham and cheese croquettes

540ml milk

¼ onion

¼ chilli

1 bay leaf

Pinch nutmeg

90g butter

90g plain flour

80g good quality strong cheese, grated (mixture of Parmesan/ mature cheddar is best)

50g cured ham (such as Serrano), diced

1 teaspoon Dijon mustard

30ml soy sauce

1½ teaspoons Worcestershire sauce

1 teaspoon sherry vinegar

Salt & pepper to taste

For the pané

150g flour

3 eggs

Bowl of Panko breadcrumbs

Make the croquette mixture by putting the milk, onion, chilli, bay leaf and nutmeg into a pan. Heat slowly, do not allow to boil.

Leave on a low temperature for 20 minutes to infuse.

We add 'cheese trim' at this stage to improve richness, so if you have any ends of Parmesan, infuse them too.

In another pan, melt the butter and stir in the flour slowly to make a roux.

Strain the milk mixture and while still hot, gradually add to the roux, whisking well between additions.

Cook on high for 15 minutes, stirring and whisking constantly to ensure there are no lumps and the mixture is silky smooth.

Add all the remaining ingredients and season with salt and pepper. Pour into a tub, cover with cling film and leave to cool completely in the fridge.

Once completely cold, roll the mixture into balls about the diameter of a 2p coin, place on greaseproof paper and refrigerate again until the balls are set.

To pané, you will need three separate bowls for the flour, whisked eggs and breadcrumbs.

A few at a time, place the ball into the flour (tap off excess), then coat in the egg and finally the breadcrumbs.

Keep them on the greaseproof paper until ready to cook – they will be at their best if you cook straight away.

Deep fry at 170°c for a couple of minutes, then finish in oven at 180°c for three minutes.

Alternatively, shallow fry in vegetable oil, turning to get an even golden colour.

Finish in the oven as above for three minutes.

Down by THE RIVER

The superb food and tranquil riverside views at the Farndon Boathouse near Newark will transport you away from the hustle and bustle of everyday life.

Follow the River Trent north towards Newark and you'll eventually come across an unexpected treasure, the lovely, leafy Farndon Boathouse Bar & Kitchen.

Opened in 2008 by the team behind Tom Brown's Brasserie at Gunthorpe and, more recently, The Riverbank at Trent Bridge, the venue oozes charm and character – with a predominantly glazed frontage and modern outdoor decked terrace providing marvellous views of an enviable rural location.

The elegant venue was created following a major refurbishment of the former New Ferry Restaurant, using a palette of natural wood cladding, stone floors, exposed beams and clever lighting.

But this great space is much more than simply a gorgeous getaway. The team here have also created a quality eatery which has won a prestigious AA Rosette, as well as being awarded a 'Certificate of Excellence' from Trip Advisor. It's also a member of UK Food & Drink 2014.

The philosophy here champions home-cooked and locally produced food. Meats, fish and cheeses are often smoked in-house and the venue also grows many of its own herbs and delicate leaves in a wonderful herb garden, situated at the back of the restaurant.

There are fantastic appetisers, starters and mains on the à la carte menu – which changes depending on the season. Sharing boards featuring antipasti of cured meat and fish are a popular choice, while the char-grill menu boasts flat iron and rib-eye steaks, the famous Boathouse gourmet burger and brilliant braised blade comprising Scotch beef, potato rosti, roasted autumn roots, smoked ham tortellini and rich beef jus.

There's also a great choice of children's meals, lovely lunches and Early Bird specials.

With a wide range of fine wines and continental beers, as well as traditional cask conditioned real ale, the Boathouse is also a popular live music venue every Sunday evening. And there are special events such as pie night and ladies' night, making it a fun and buzzing choice throughout the year.

Farndon Boathouse's
THAI FISH BOWL

One of the restaurant's most popular dishes, which has been on the menu for
six years – swap the fish ingredients to chicken or vegetables as desired.
Serves four.

Ingredients

For the vegetables

1 small onion

4 cloves garlic

50g fresh ginger, diced

2 lemongrass stalks, bashed

2 fresh chillies including seeds

4 kaffir lime leaves

100ml double cream

300ml coconut milk

2 teaspoons red Thai paste

For the fish

400g salmon

400g hake or cod

10 mussels in shell

16 king prawns

16 crayfish tails

To finish

Zest & juice of 1 lime

4 sprigs fresh coriander

250g cooked rice noodles

150g crispy fried egg noodles

Micro coriander cress

Sesame oil

Method

Sweat all of the vegetable ingredients in a thick bottomed pan without colouring the vegetables or the pan base.

Add the cream and reduce for 5-8 minutes.

Now add the coconut milk and the Thai paste, bring to the boil and simmer for 15-20 minutes to infuse all flavours together.

Season to taste, then once happy with the flavour, pass off all the vegetables.

Return the liquid back to the pan and finish with lime juice and zest. Season and taste.

Add the chunks of fish to the sauce and when it returns to a simmer, add the shellfish.

Simmer for another 2-4 minutes before adding the rice noodles. Finish with freshly chopped coriander.

Serve in a hot bowl with deep fried crispy noodles (if you don't have a fryer, simply cook off the egg noodles prior, and place on greaseproof paper in the oven for 45-50 minutes on 160°c).

Put a few sprigs of micro coriander on top and drizzle with a little sesame oil.

Done!

A Pizza THE ACTION

Fire & Ice is the fashionable wood-fired eatery and wine bar which was there at the very beginning of the boom in West Bridgford's food and drink scene.

It was 2006 when Fire & Ice first opened in the centre of stylish West Bridgford as a family-run affair.

Little did anyone know that this laid-back lounge bar specialising in great pizzas, burgers, pasta and surf and turf, largely prepared inside the amazing brick oven centrepiece, would help kick-start a new era in the town's food and drink economy.

"There was nothing like it here at the time – a venue where local people could have dinner, a drink and a dance. And where Fire & Ice went, so many others have now followed."

The menu is quite comprehensive, offering an amazing selection of wood-fired pizzas created by hand from twice-proven dough.

Toppings range from classics such as meat feast and Margherita to more unusual options, like Florentine (a mix of spinach, egg and black olives) or Quack – featuring BBQ sauce, crispy duck, hoisin sauce, spring onion and cucumber.

Delicious smoked haddock fishcakes are a new addition, with mouth-watering pan-fried sea bass and traditional lasagne, cooked in that amazing oven, along with other tempting dishes.

With the longest bar in Bridgford, Fire & Ice also provides the very best in totally original cocktails including a number of witty Nottingham-inspired reinterpretations of more familiar recipes. There is also a wide choice of wines, Champagnes and beers, whilst regular live music helps create a buzzing, celebratory atmosphere.

Fire & Ice's
MEXICO PIZZA

This classically fiery pizza makes eight medium sized thin pizzas – great for sharing.

Ingredients

For the pizza dough

1kg Capputo '00' flour

14g fresh yeast

1 teaspoon fine sea salt

2 tablespoons extra virgin olive oil

650ml lukewarm water

For the tomato base

2 tablespoons olive oil

1 large onion, chopped

1 clove garlic, crushed

400g chopped tomatoes

2 teaspoons brown sugar

2 teaspoons dried oregano

Fresh basil leaves

Salt and freshly ground black pepper

For the basil pesto

30g fresh basil leaves

2 tablespoons extra virgin olive oil

10g pine nuts

Freshly ground black pepper and sea salt to taste

Quantities to your liking

Buffalo mozzarella

Cooked chicken

Sweetcorn

Mixed peppers

Fresh basil pesto

Method

For the pizza dough

Mix together the fresh yeast, water and olive oil and leave for a few minutes.

Sieve the flour and salt onto a clean work surface and make a well in the middle. Pour in the wet ingredients above and, using a fork, gradually bring in the flour until it comes together. Then rub your hands in some flour and work the ingredients together until you have a smooth, springy dough.

Roll into a ball and place in a large, flour coated bowl, sprinkle some flour on top. Then cover the bowl with a damp cloth and put in a warm place until the dough has doubled in size (approximately two hours).

Sprinkle the work surface with some flour and knead the dough ball to push the air out. Divide the dough into 8 balls and roll them out. Leave for about 10 minutes (heat your oven at this stage to about 220°c), and then start with your toppings.

For the tomato base

Heat the oil in a saucepan and gently cook the onion and garlic until softened. Stir in the tomatoes, oregano and sugar. Bring to a simmer and cook slowly for 45 minutes to 1 hour. Stir in the basil and season with salt and pepper. Blend in a food processor until smooth.

For the basil pesto

Blitz all the ingredients in a food processor until smooth.

Open the dough balls and either using a rolling pin or pulling by hand, stretch out to approximately 12 inch diameter. Spoon a thin layer of tomato sauce over each pizza base, sprinkle over a large handful of grated mozzarella, add sliced mixed peppers, chopped and diced, cooked chicken breast and a handful of sweetcorn kernels. Place on a heated baking tray or pizza stone into the oven for approximately 10 minutes.

When crisp and bubbling, remove from the oven and scatter over torn basil leaves.

Fire & Ice's
FABULOUS COCKTAIL CREATIONS

Raise a glass with bar manager Emma Tirel's wonderful Bridgford Donkey (a Nottingham twist on the classic Moscow Mule) or a grilled Peach Julep, based on a traditional julep. Serves one.

Ingredients

For the Bridgford Donkey

50ml Absolut Vodka infused with hibiscus flowers

15ml fresh lime juice

10ml sugar syrup (2:1 sugar to water)

5ml pomegranate syrup (grenadine)

2 dashes of Fee Brothers rhubarb bitters (available online and at Marks and Spencer's)

Fever Tree ginger beer

For the Peach Julep

60ml Wild Turkey 81 Bourbon

12 mint leaves

10ml orange blossom honey syrup

4 peaches, cut in half

Brown sugar

Crushed ice

Method

Bridgford Donkey:

For the infused vodka (makes 700ml)

Pour a bottle of Absolut Vodka into a kilner jar, and add roughly three handfuls of dried hibiscus flowers. These are easily available over the internet and at food health stores.

Leave the flowers sitting according to your personal preference – the longer you leave them and the more you use, the more flavoursome the vodka becomes. We leave ours for two hours, as we find bitter notes may take over after this time.

Put the lid tightly on the jar and let it sit (place away from direct sunlight) until the vodka takes on the desired flavour.

Drain the dried flowers out of the vodka, using a sieve if desired (wash immediately afterwards), and funnel back into the bottle.

Shake the first five ingredients with cubed ice and strain into an ice-filled glass.

Top up with ginger beer and stir.

Garnish with a lime wedge and hibiscus flower.

TIP: *If you don't have a cocktail shaker and strainer at home, try using an empty sports drink bottle, or travel mug or shake in a jam jar and pour through a sieve.*

Peach Julep:

For the grilled peach syrup (makes 200ml)

Cut four peaches in half and dip the cut halves in brown sugar.

Grill them on a medium heat, cut side down, until they are caramelised.

After they cool, purée them to your desired "thickness" in a blender and mix with 2:1 sugar, until it forms a syrupy consistency.

Keep in an airtight container in the fridge for up to four days.

Shake all ingredients with cubed ice and strain into julep cup, half filled with crushed ice.

Stir the drink with the crushed ice.

Top up the cup with more crushed ice and stir again.

Repeat this process until the drink fills the cup.

Garnish with a mint sprig.

TIP: *To make crushed ice at home, put ice cubes into a bag and smash with a rolling pin.*

Fran's LAMB TAGINE

Frances Finn has been a broadcaster in Nottingham for more than ten years. A regular on BBC Radio Nottingham since 2003 and now the face of Notts TV, she hosts news programmes, chat shows, and the weekly Channel 8 Debate.

You can also find her on Radio 2 and 5 Live.

Fran has a husband who is a marvellous cook and a little girl who loves to help out in the kitchen – although the amount of cake mix they prepare never quite seems to make it into the cake tin!

Big on food that is full of flavour, Fran loves spices and fresh herbs and has no time for meals that are all style and no substance. But she enjoys experimenting with a bit of fancy presentation from time to time – and this favourite dish is "dead easy to present, and never goes wrong!"

Serves four hungry people.

Ingredients

900g diced lamb leg or shoulder (mutton also good, but cook for twice as long)

1 tablespoon plain flour

1 large onion, roughly chopped

4 cloves garlic, finely chopped

Fresh ginger, finely chopped

1 tin chopped tomatoes

1 glass red wine

2 apples or pears or a mix of both, peeled, cored and diced

Large handful of raisins or sultanas

1 dessertspoon honey

15-20 black pitted olives

1 tablespoon ground cumin

1 teaspoon chilli powder

1 teaspoon ground coriander

1 cinnamon stick or cassia bark, or 2 teaspoons ground cinnamon

1 teaspoon salt

Small bunch of fresh coriander

Handful of whole almonds (optional)

Couscous as per instructions on packaging

Method

Soften the onions, garlic and ginger in a saucepan, or hob-friendly casserole dish, on a medium heat.

Coat the lamb in the flour. Try putting it in a carrier bag and giving it a good shake.

Add the lamb to the pan and fry until it has colour. Don't stir too often to give the meat chance to brown up.

Add the tomatoes and red wine. Add all the spices, honey, salt and cinnamon.

Add the fruit and sultanas/raisins and olives. Stir and bring to the boil.

Transfer to a casserole dish and cook for 1½ hours at 160°c.

The lamb is cooked when it is really tender. Carry on cooking if it is not (shoulder may need a little longer).

When done, remove the cinnamon or cassia. If you want to add the crunch of some whole almonds, put them in a dry frying pan and heat until they brown a little. Add them before you serve.

Add coriander before serving. Also mix coriander with the couscous, along with a teaspoon of olive oil.

To serve

Make the couscous into a dome in the centre of a plate using a ramekin or tea cup, greased with olive oil.

Serve the tagine around the couscous. If you drip on the edges of the plate, wipe clean with a kitchen towel.

Quality runs in THE FAMILY

Fred Hallam Ltd on Beeston High Road has been serving the town since 1908. A proud retailer of the finest fruit and vegetables, it's also a specialist fishmongers with something for every taste.

A visit to Fred Hallam's in Beeston is more than a regular shopping experience – it's actually a fascinating journey taking in the proud retail heritage of Nottingham.

The walls at this High Road fishmongers and fruit shop are full of brilliant original photographs telling the story of a much-loved business from Edwardian times to the present day.

Raised in an orphanage, Fred Hallam started out hawking fruit from a barrow from an early age. After many years of hard graft he managed to buy the premises at 23 High Road Beeston, next to the busy Palace cinema.

Fred's son John took on the business next and spent a lifetime at the helm before passing it on to his own son, also called Fred. It was he who converted the premises into a modern self-service shop in the 1980's in line with changing shopping habits brought on by the rise of the supermarket. Sons Miles and Andy Hallam are now the fourth generation to run this thriving enterprise, employing a staff of 25.

Miles and Andy are passionate about supporting the local community, backing local sports teams, school projects and charity events. They also supply to local catering firms, restaurants, schools and nursing homes with everything from the basics to micro herbs and rare mushrooms.

The store has had a number of facelifts and extensions over the decades, creating a larger retail area as well as a new food preparation kitchen to the rear. This great space is where Hallam's in-house chef prepares a host of fresh treats – such as pâtés, fish pies and fresh soups. Other notable goodies include pressed juices from Starkey's fruit farm, Melton Mowbray pork pies, award winning cheeses, dairy and quality Italian olives.

The day here starts at 3:30am, six days a week – the brothers travelling to Nottingham market to hand pick the best produce available – while deliveries from other suppliers arrive at dawn.

"Most of our fish is sourced responsibly from sustainable fisheries-mainly in Cornwall. One fishery in particular use traditional and environmentally friendly methods to catch a huge variety of fish for our counter. The fish has often been landed the day before it arrives to us by courier.

"We try to offer only the freshest catch and would rather offer an alternative than stock varieties which are out of season or have been unethically fished by methods such as dredging.

"We are passionate about protecting our industry and that's why we believe that responsible fishing not only rests with the fisherman but with the fishmonger and consumer too."

Changes in the business in recent years, combined with the fresh new ideas and the sheer enthusiasm of the latest generation to run this family affair, have ensured Hallam's will continue to proudly serve the good folk of Beeston for many years to come.

Finest fresh Brancaster mussels from the Thomas Large family on the Norfolk coast.

In season from September to source our tasty mussels directly

Brancaster Mussels Kilo or kg for £5.00

www.fredhallam.com

STARKEY'S GREEN JUICE FROM SOUTHWELL

DISCOVERY APPLE & STRAWBERRY £3.99 (500ml)

ORIGINAL BRAMLEY APPLE JUICE £3.25

£1.50

£2.25

BRAMLEY APPLE & BLACKBERRY JUICE 500ml

Brancaster Mussels

SWEET & JUICY NECTARINES 1kg BOX £1.50

SWEET JUICY NAVEL ORANGES £1.50

£1.50

£1.25

RASPBERRIES 79£ 2 for £1.50

FRESH FI 4 for £1.

ILSA

NORFOLK EASY SCRAPERS 45 Plb 99 Pkg

FISH FRED HALLAM LTD.

BEST HERRINGS ARBROATH SMOKIES

BEST COD FILLETS 1.70

BEST PLAICE FILLETS 1.80

BEST COD ROES

FRESH RAINBOW TROUT

Fred Hallam's
BRANCASTER MUSSELS
IN STARKEY'S BRAMLEY JUICE

Thomas Large and family have been harvesting these tasty Norfolk mussels in Brancaster for over a generation. We've combined this classic French recipe with a twist of our own, by using a great locally produced pressed Bramley apple juice from Starkey's Fruit Farm in Southwell, home of the original Bramley apple seedling tree.

Every ingredient in this recipe is available in our store. Fresh mussels are available from October to March, so visit us today and try this tasty recipe with some other great British food heroes! Serves two.

Ingredients

1kg fresh Brancaster mussels

2 tablespoons olive oil

4 banana shallots, finely chopped

2 smoked garlic cloves, chopped

Small knob of butter

2 sticks celery, thinly sliced

250ml bottle Starkey's pressed Bramley juice

Small bunch flat leaf parsley, chopped

Juice of half a lemon

Crusty bread, to serve

Method

Clean the mussels by thoroughly scrubbing them under plenty of running water, pulling away the 'beards', the seaweed-like stringy threads.

Discard any broken mussels along with the 'beards', and any mussels that don't close tightly when you tap them.

Heat the olive oil in a heavy pan with a tight-fitting lid. Add the shallots and smoked garlic and cook over a medium heat until softened, but not coloured.

Add the celery with a knob of butter for a further minute until combined, then add the mussels and the bottle of Bramley juice to the pan.

Turn the heat down to low. Put the lid on the pan, shake, and allow the mussels to steam. Cook for about 4-5 minutes, lifting the lid from time to time to check – you will know they are cooked when the shells have opened. Discard any mussels that remain closed.

Finish off with the chopped parsley and a squeeze of half a lemon and serve straight away with crusty bread.

Down on THE FARM

A visit to multi-award winning Gonalston Farm Shop is a uniquely exhilarating culinary experience.

It was 2003 when farmers Georgina and Ross Mason first opened Gonalston Farm Shop near Lowdham – with a simple mission to provide the local community with the freshest meat and highest quality produce.

The couple, who come from a long farming tradition, have a no-nonsense 'straight from field to plate' philosophy and it's a view that has seen their venture win widespread acclaim both in Nottingham and nationally, with accolades such as runner-up for the Great Taste Shop of the Year – twice! Along with many other awards.

All the beef sold at this famed foodie paradise is home reared on the farm, while tasty lamb and pork are also sourced from nearby.

The premium quality produce here is prepared and hung by a team of master butchers in the impressive in-house butchery, with an amazing meat counter that seems to stretch for miles.

Gonalston also has an excellent in-store fishmongers specialising in fresh line-caught fish and shellfish from the south coast, as well as a great selection of smoked fish.

Seasonality and traceability are always of huge importance.

Alongside all this, a range of other fresh foods are available daily, including seasonal fruits and vegetables complemented by the finest preserves, cakes and condiments.

The excellent delicatessen is stocked with an enviable selection of mouth-watering goodies from handmade cheeses to plump olives. And the grocery section is literally overflowing with delicious home prepared ready meals, ingredients from far and wide, biscuits, crackers and exotic organic chocolates.

There are also tempting fine wines, speciality beers and country ciders, alongside an array of stylish gift ideas, such as wonderful personalised hampers.

Gonalston is particularly proud of its '50 mile campaign' which promotes the use of locally sourced produce. It means that the food has travelled or been produced within 50 miles of Gonalston Farm, so you know the food is as fresh and nutritious as possible.

Look out for the '50 mile' sticker on products.

Gonalston Farm Shop's

COTE DE BOEUF

Georgina uses an Aga to cook this mouth-watering classic. Serves four-six

Ingredients

A two rib 28 day dry aged cote de boeuf joint, French trimmed at room temperature (weight around 1.5kg)

Salt and pepper

For the gravy

1 tablespoon plain flour

Good quality beef stock

1-2 tablespoons Marsala

Method

Heat the oven to around 200°c.

Pop the meat in an oven and hob proof pan, as after it has been removed from the oven you'll use it to make the gravy.

Rub black pepper and a little salt into the skin of the meat and sit it in the pan skin side up, so its two bones are against the bottom of the pan.

Place in the oven for 15 minutes per 500g for rare cooked (with no extra time) or 20 minutes for medium rare, 30 minutes for well done.

Reduce the heat to 180°c after 15 minutes.

Take the meat from the oven, place it onto a warm plate, cover with tin foil and leave it to rest for the time it takes to cook any vegetables you are having.

The bigger the joint, the longer the rest. During this time the meat relaxes, and lovely juices will run from the joint. Save this for the gravy.

For the gravy

Scrape any residue off the bottom of the meat pan with a wooden spoon.

Add a tablespoon of plain flour and gradually mix in any meat juices from the cooked resting joint, followed by a good quality beef stock.

Top up with water from the cooked vegetables, a little at a time over a high heat, constantly stirring to avoid lumps.

To finish, add a little Marsala, bubble and stir until thickened.

There you have it – and I promise this should taste amazing!

Straight from
THE HART

Hart's is the pioneering restaurant that brought ambitious dining to Nottingham city centre for the very first time back in 1997.

Tim Hart had been a successful hotelier, restaurateur and entrepreneur for many years before he brought a taste of the high life to Nottingham with the launch of his own restaurant in 1997.

Having run award-winning Hambleton Hall in Rutland since 1980, he was "nagged" into opening Hart's by numerous Nottingham-based clients.

At the time, Tim felt the city centre was lacking an ambitious restaurant, and he made it his mission to bring us fine dining at affordable prices.

With the perfect venue inside beautiful old buildings at Standard Hill, the site of Nottingham's former General Hospital, the team were very much food pioneers. They cleverly tapped into a new mood, providing high quality cuisine to discerning local people.

Tim was determined that his own restaurant would follow the same philosophy as Hambleton Hall – offering classical combinations of flavours and ingredients, with nothing flash or showy.

Respect for ingredients and using locally sourced produce where possible, is key. A thoroughly professional blend of skilled service and modern British cooking in a stylish and comfortable interior, that's the no-nonsense story here.

Tim has a strong team to bring it all together, with head chef Dan Burridge and General Manager Sally Martin leading a smooth operation. Hart's is also constantly evolving to reflect what they know about their customers.

Typical starters today range from gin and tonic cured salmon to roast wood pigeon, whilst mains include lamb shoulder, whole baby plaice or pistachio gnocchi with pumpkin purée. Desserts such as ginger sponge, chocolate fondant and quince soufflé complete the picture.

With Hart's Hotel opening in 2002, and a complete restaurant refurbishment masterminded by Tim's wife Stefa in 2006, the venue continues to inspire and grow.

Tim says: "Our basic philosophy hasn't changed, but the city has – and we will move forward to bring fresh ideas to the fore whenever we can."

Hart's

Hart's
COLWICK CHEESECAKE WITH ITALIAN MERINGUE

One of the chef's favourite desserts, using a wonderful local ingredient.
Serves six.

Ingredients

For the cheesecake

250g Colwick cheese

63g sugar

20g flour

½ vanilla pod

½ zest lemon

1½ eggs

70g crème fraiche

13g cocoa butter

½ bronze gelatine leaf, soaked

For the Italian meringue

100g sugar

100g egg white

30g water

For the oat shortbread

137g oats

50g flour

75g sugar

1g bicarbonate of soda

1.5g salt

112g cold butter

For the figs and reduction

8 ripe black figs

1 lime

1 cinnamon stick

3 star anise

2 whole cloves

500ml orange juice

500ml red wine

125ml honey

25ml grenadine

Zest of 1 lemon

400g lemon

400g sugar

Port and brandy to taste

Method

For the cheesecake

Mix all the ingredients together in a food processor.

Place in a small tray covered with aluminium foil and cook in the oven at 140°c for 25 minutes until set.

Remove from oven and blend in a food processor, adding the gelatine leaf. Set to one side.

For the Italian meringue

Boil the water and sugar until it reaches 118°c.

Whisk the egg whites with an electric mixer until the meringue has developed.

Slow the mixer down, leave on the lowest setting and then slowly add the hot sugar syrup.

Keep whisking slowly until the meringue has cooled (this usually takes 10-15 minutes).

Fold the meringue into the cheesecake mix, pour into a tray and place into the fridge to set.

For the oat shortbread

Blend the oats, flour, sugar, soda and salt together.

Add butter in three stages until just combined, pulsing each time.

Roll and bake at 175°c for 15 minutes. Once cooked, cut into desired shapes.

For the figs and reduction

Bring all the ingredients to the boil, simmer for five minutes then take off the heat.

Drop the figs in the liquid and leave for 5 minutes. Take out and pass and reduce the liquid.

Arrange the elements on a plate. Garnish with (roast walnuts, celery cut into small batons, celery leaves, apple cut into matchstick size strips, grapes halved and lightly poached figs.)

It tastes better when it's
HOMEMADE

Homemade is the cosy Hockley café that's expanded into two other fabulous Nottingham venues.

Creating a warm and friendly home from home feel in her business comes very naturally to Jasmin Barlow-Wilkinson, owner of award-winning café bistro Homemade.

The original venue, which opened back in 2005, was her attempt at recreating the same "proper" food and laid back atmosphere she'd been so used to at home – having grown up amongst a family of real Nottingham foodies.

Jasmin was four when she first remembers learning the ropes in the kitchen alongside her Auntie Flo and granny (who, by all accounts, made the world's best ever chips). This then continued into her teenage years cooking with her god-mother Helen.

After going on to do a degree in hospitality and business, she realised that the hotel-oriented nature of the studies was not really for her and she ended up moving into HR.

But after a period spent travelling and picking up a plethora of inspiring new food ideas, Jasmin returned with a fresh determination to open her own eatery.

The whole ethos of Homemade, in Pelham Street, was to move away from the stuffy fine dining/fusion food craze *en vogue* in the early part of the Millennium. She'd been used to having friends pile round to her place at the weekend while she cooked real wholesome food for them – and that's exactly what she wanted inside her new café.

With a big emphasis on local suppliers – most are within three miles of the café – Jasmin's menus are still filled with tempting choices, such as the "Posh Pants Brekkie" with smoked salmon and scrambled eggs, fish finger sandwiches, squash and goat's cheese salad, homemade burgers, quesadillas and fresh fish dishes.

Meanwhile, cakes have taken on a life of their own with Homemade. Taking inspiration from the lavish window displays at trendy London venues such as Choccywoccydoodah and Ottolenghi, Jasmin created her own tempting version – and Nottingham went mad for it.

Now, not only does the café have a lunchtime rush from noon to 2pm, it also has a cake rush mid-afternoon as sweet-toothed obsessives clamour for their fix of delicious brownies, blueberry cake, carrot cakes and Victoria sponges.

Raspberry & Lemon Cake

the Homemade brasnie

This happy state of affairs at Homemade would probably have continued, but little did Jasmin know that her café was about to "accidentally" branch out into other parts of Nottingham too.

The Sherwood venue opened out of the blue in 2012 when the owner of A Room Full of Butterflies gift shop in Mansfield Road asked if Jasmin would like to run a café at the rear of the premises. Initially Jasmin thought this was a wind up, unable to think of a good enough reason why not, the expansion began.

Then in 2013, Nottingham City Council unveiled its multi-million pound refurbishment of The Pavilion at Forest Recreation Ground and asked Homemade's outside catering team to do the food at the launch.

Jasmin's pop-up café went down a storm and when the council suggested she should apply for the tender to run the site permanently, she eventually did – and won it. Now this beautiful new space has provided a whole new opportunity for the business, including weddings and larger functions.

"We're not going to be taking on the world with a big chain of Homemade cafés though," Jasmin laughs. "I think that would lose the magic."

Nevertheless, she admits, Homemade has become a sort of brand. Even though all the sites are very different, there's something about the cute bunting, chalkboards and table layouts that lets you know exactly where you're eating.

The menus are also a constant – although ideas are mixed up a little, with some things working in the city centre, but not in Forest Fields and vice versa.

Alongside head chef Mike Haywood, who's in charge at Hockley, Jasmin and Mike ensure their menus are flavoursome and interesting, with the introduction of many Latin and French flavours to the dishes which are proving very popular.

As well as outside catering, Homemade is also a regular at all the big local festivals and events, including Splendour, the Nottingham Beer Festival and Goose Fair.

It's a winning mix that has seen the eatery win runner up prizes in the Observer Food Awards no less than three times, while it was also voted one of the top independent businesses of the year by the Nottingham BID (Business Improvement District). All this wouldn't have been possible without their great team of 'Homemaders' – the staff work their socks off to help create cafés we're proud of.

Jasmin's Cajun Chicken
QUESADILLAS WITH HOMEMADE GUACAMOLE

A yummy Homemade tortilla dish, ideal for sharing with friends as a snack.
Serves three-four people as snacks, or two for a supper.

Ingredients

For the quesadillas

4 soft flour tortillas (supermarket own brand ones are usually the best quality)

200g grated Cheddar

200g grated mozzarella block

Roasted peppers, chopped (Homemade ones are easy enough to make, but you can also buy them ready roasted in supermarkets too)

10 baby plum tomatoes, finely chopped

½ red onion, finely diced

Coriander, chopped

Fresh red chilli, finely sliced

Cracked black pepper

2 chicken breast fillets, diced

Blackened Cajun seasoning

Olive oil

For the guacamole

3 ripe avocados

½ red onion, finely diced

½ teaspoon dried chilli flakes

5 baby plum tomatoes, finely chopped

Juice of 1 lime

2 crushed garlic cloves

Glug of extra virgin olive oil

Maldon salt

Cracked black pepper

Fresh coriander, chopped

Method

In a bowl, mix the Cajun seasoning with some olive oil to make a marinade and pour over the chicken fillet. Set aside in the fridge for an hour.

Meanwhile, make the guacamole by scooping out the ripe avocado using a tablespoon into a separate mixing bowl. You should have rough big chunks of avocado.

Add all of the other guacamole ingredients and mix with a tablespoon, avoiding mashing it into a paste. You should end up with half smooth, half rough smaller chunks of avocado.

Place your finished guacamole into a serving dish and garnish with a little fresh coriander and set aside.

Prepare the quesadilla cheese mix in a separate bowl. Mix together the grated cheeses, tomatoes, onions, peppers, chilli flakes, black pepper and coriander. You should end up with a colourful looking cheese mix.

In a frying pan over a medium heat, cook the marinated chicken fillet until the meat has turned white all the way through. Once cooked, shred the chicken while hot, ready to go inside the tortillas.

Place one of your tortillas on a chopping board. On one half, add the cheese mix in a semi circle, then sprinkle the shredded chicken over the top.

Once you have a semi circle of filling, fold over your tortilla, sandwiching and flattening it with the palm of your hands. Repeat this process with the remaining tortillas.

Then in a dry, large non stick frying pan, place two of your semi circle tortilla parcels over a medium heat. Cook for approx 5-6 minutes each side, until the tortilla starts to golden and becomes slightly crispy.

Chop each cooked quesadilla into three triangles and stack up on a board. Serve with the guacamole and scoff away!

Jasmin's Peanut Butter
BANANA & CHOCOLATE CHIP CAKE

Serves ten.

Ingredients

For the cake

250g softened salted butter (you can use unsalted too, but you'll need to add a pinch of salt)

250g soft brown sugar

300g self raising flour

4 eggs

250g crunchy peanut butter

1 tablespoon vanilla extract

2 ripe bananas, mashed

150g dark chocolate chips

For the buttercream

150g soft butter

200g icing sugar

50g best quality dark cocoa

100g dark chocolate, melted

70g crunchy peanut butter

100g bag of dry roasted peanuts

Method

For the cake

Preheat the oven to 170°c and line two 23cm sandwich cake tins.

Using an electric hand whisk, whip up the butter to a smooth, rich looking consistency. Then slowly whisk in the soft brown sugar.

Whisk in the eggs and vanilla extract together.

Using a sieve, add half the flour, followed by half the egg mixture. Mix with the hand whisk.

Do the same again with the remaining flour, adding in the rest of the egg mixture until smooth.

Add the peanut butter and the mashed bananas and whisk into the mixture. Fold in the chocolate chips with a wooden spoon.

Distribute the mix evenly between the two baking tins, spreading it out with a palette knife or the back of a spoon as necessary. Place in the oven to cook for approx 35 minutes.

Once cooked, remove from the oven, leaving the cakes in the tins to cool down for a good hour before icing.

For the buttercream icing

Whisk up the butter, then add the icing sugar using a sieve and whisk to a smooth consistency.

Add the peanut butter, cocoa and melted chocolate and whisk up together.

This buttercream will be going into the centre of the cake as the sandwich filling and also on the top.

Once the cake is iced, sprinkle the top of the cake with dry roasted peanuts for decoration.

Spanish HIGHS

The rustic simplicity of Spanish tapas is fused with the experience of a fine dining restaurant at Iberico World Tapas.

The team behind Nottingham's award-winning World Service restaurant brought their vision for a more laid-back dining experience to the city back in 2007.

Iberico World Tapas encompassed a style of food which was already incredibly popular, but injected a bold new twist – mingling richly exotic Spanish flavours and ingredients with much lighter Pan Asian influences.

Housed inside the visually stunning Grade II listed Galleries of Justice, the authentic bodega styling and cave-like dining area creates a fabulous social atmosphere as customers share dishes and enjoy exciting new taste experiences.

The restaurant was once again awarded the coveted Bib Gourmand accolade in the 2015 Michelin Guide, recognising exceptional food at reasonable prices. It's one of only 150 establishments in the UK to receive such an honour – and the only one in Nottingham.

Jacque Ferreira and Simon Carlin front the team at Iberico and this recognition means more than even the very top food critics' award as it shows that they've created great food which is accessible to everyone.

The Express Dining menu here is littered with inspirational choices from jamon croquetas and baked Cornish mussels to mushroom carpaccio and spinach and goat's cheese piquillo peppers.

Meanwhile the main food menu offers something for all tastes, with award-winning hams, and chorizo, accompanied by bread, nibbles, pickles and olives, as well as Paleta Iberico de Bellota Reserva – an incredible tasting cured meat made from black footed Iberico pigs, descended from wild boars.

With superb wines and sherries to choose from, this stylish venue is Moorish in more ways than one!

Iberico's
CRISPY PORK BELLY
WITH BRAMLEY APPLE MUSTARD AND MORCILLA

A delicious dish from the Mediterranean including wonderful crackling and Spanish black pudding. Serves four.

Ingredients

700g free-range pork belly

250g table salt

250g caster sugar

2½ litres water

2 Bramley apples, cored and chopped

½ tablespoon Dijon mustard

120g Morcilla cooking sausage (Spanish black pudding)

Pork belly skin (available from your butcher)

Rapeseed oil for deep frying the crackling

French watercress to garnish

80ml chicken wing jus

Method

For the pork belly

Mix the salt, sugar and water in a saucepan and gently heat to dissolve.

Remove from the heat and cool completely.

Scour the skin of the pork belly with a very sharp knife or razor blade.

Submerge the belly in the brine for 24 hours. Remove the belly from the brine and pat dry.

Vacuum pack the belly on high and cook "sous vide" for 48 hours at 62°c (this method of cooking meat slowly in an airtight plastic bag in a water bath at a controlled temperature ensures even cooking and retains moisture).

When cooked, remove from the water bath and submerge in ice water for 90 minutes to cool below 3°c.

If you don't have use of a water bath and vacuum pack machine, you could pat the belly dry after brining it and roast it a preheated oven at 240°c, for 30 minutes and then for a further hour at 150°c.

Now press the belly under a chopping board with a weight placed on top in the fridge overnight.

Portion the belly into four 170g pieces. It is now ready to be pan-fried, skin side down, then placed in the oven skin side down at 180°c for about 6-8 minutes until crispy and golden.

For the Bramley apple mustard

Sweat the chopped apples with two tablespoons of water in a small saucepan.

Cook the apples until you are able to mash with a spoon. Transfer to a blender and add the mustard. Blend until silky smooth.

For the crackling

Submerge the pork skin in cold water in a large saucepan.

Bring it to the boil. Once it is boiling, turn down the heat to simmer for about 2-3 hours. Keep the skin submerged.

Remove from the water and scrape off any excess fat from under the skin.

Dehydrate at 60°c for 10-12 hours on a cooling rack. The skin should be hard like plastic if dried correctly.

Once dried, you can break it into smaller pieces and deep fry at 200°c for about 45 seconds. It should puff up after about ten seconds.

Drain on a paper towel and season with salt.

For the Morcilla

Remove the sausage casing and pan fry on medium heat until cooked through.

Drain on paper towel.

You are now ready to assemble all the elements.

Smoke KING

Local legend Johnny Pusztai has brought a passion for quality produce to JT Beedham and Sons Butchers in Sherwood.

The preparation and cooking of meat is a genuine art form for Johnny Pusztai, the colourful curator in charge of award-winning JT Beedham and Sons, in Sherwood.

The butcher's boy turned proprietor has been at the helm of this amazing emporium since 1991, having started out as a Saturday lad at the shop – originally founded in 1884.

His passion and enthusiasm for the highest quality produce and traditional preparation methods undoubtedly come from his Hungarian roots – his refugee father Dezso having settled in Sherwood in the 1950s.

Growing up in a family who built their own smokehouse to cure and smoke bacon and gammon for traditional Hungarian salamis clearly left a huge legacy.

The enormous smoker in the back yard at Beedham's forms the centre of operations at this unique establishment, with locally sourced bacon, duck, chicken, mutton and sausages all cured and smoked over oak chippings for 24 hours. Lit every Friday, the tempting smell wafts over Sherwood to entice weekend shoppers.

With 25 varieties of sausage on offer alone, the butchers is bursting with exotic ideas and delicacies from curried sausage to Hungarian Kolbasz, a spicy salami reminiscent of chorizo with lashings of pork and paprika (the exact recipe is, of course, a strictly guarded secret).

The top-notch meats, offal, burgers and poultry have won numerous awards, while Johnny himself has received glowing reviews from leading food writers, made regular TV appearances and has produced his own quirky videos conveying his love for his work.

A former ice hockey player who once made centre for Nottingham Panthers, Johnny and his team continue to spread the message far and wide, regularly appearing at a host of major food events and shows throughout the UK.

Expect the Sausage King of Nottingham to reign supreme for many years to come.

JT Beedham's
PORK PORKOLT

A tasty take on the traditional Hungarian goulash, reflecting Johnny Pusztai's rich food heritage – use chicken, beef or lamb as an alternative if you prefer. Serves four.

Ingredients

800g pork (leg or shoulder)

1 large onion

1 clove garlic

2-3 bell peppers (capsicum)

1 large tomato

4 tablespoons oil

1 tablespoon ground paprika

Salt and ground black pepper

1 bell pepper and sour cream for garnishing

Method

Cut the meat into 2cm cubes.

Finely chop the onion. Seed and chop the peppers. Cut the tomato into eight pieces.

Sauté the onion slowly in the oil and remove from the heat. Add the garlic, peppers and meat and return to the heat.

Cook for a few minutes, stirring continuously. Season with salt, then add the paprika and pieces of tomato.

Cover and leave to cook in its own juices for at least 1 hour and 20 minutes.

Replace any juices that evaporate with a little warm water if necessary to make a thick sauce.

Garnish the cooked dish with the sliced pepper and sour cream.

Serve with dumplings, pasta pellets, home baked bread, a fresh salad or preserved vegetables.

The true
TASTE OF INDIA

Kayal is the Hockley restaurant that has brought the distinctive flavours of Kerala cuisine to Nottingham.

For more than 2,000 years, people have been travelling to the Kerala region of South West India to trade goods, creating a wealth of unusual and inspiring food traditions.

And the rich heritage of this unusual cuisine has been brought to vivid life at quality restaurant Kayal, which opened in Broad Street in 2007.

This lovely eatery is a world away from typical curry houses, offering unique food that's very distinctive in flavour, with a big emphasis on seafood.

It's the brainchild of Jaimon Thomas, a former maître d' who has worked at many five star hotels and travelled the world on luxurious cruise ships. On his return to the UK in 2005, he opened his first Kerala restaurant in Leicester – and his Nottingham venue followed a few years later.

Cooking here is all about tradition, aromas and spices. Dishes are mildly flavoured and gently cooked, with a great range of vegetables, meats and seafood containing a pungent flavour heightened by tamarind. It's also extremely healthy fare.

Chefs at this family-run business are born and bred in the Kerala region and have been steeped in the tradition. Expect a melange of aromas made up of pepper, cardamom, cloves, turmeric, ginger, chillies and mustard. The team have even helped Hairy Bikers Simon King and Dave Myers cook authentic Kerala dishes.

As well as a great range of starters and pre-meal pickles, menu highlights include Njandu curry featuring fresh crab cooked in authentic spices and coconut sauce, as well as the restaurant's signature dish Cheera Erachi curry, with tender pieces of lamb cooked in fresh spinach, turmeric, red chillies and onions.

Don't miss the "from the garden" offerings, bursting with superb vegetarian stews, curries and spicy delights. Throughout the day, you can also enjoy the delicious Kayal lunch tiffin or special afternoon teas.

This is a place where wonderful ancient food traditions meet modern service and quality.

Kayal

Kayal's HERB DOSA

A tasty traditional pancake dish with Masala stuffing – ideal for sharing.
Serves two.

Ingredients

For the batter
100g spinach

100g basil

5g coriander leaves

500g basmati rice

250g black lentils

5g fenugreek

For the masala stuffing
150g yam, diced

75g colocasia

1 onion, sliced

10g ginger

10g green chilli

50g boiled potatoes, mashed

To garnish
Gooseberry chutney

Apple chutney

Method

For the batter

Soak the rice and lentils separately over six hours in water and grind both to a paste with the spinach, basil, fenugreek and coriander leaves.

Mix both pastes together and add salt and water to make a batter.

Leave the batter at room temperature overnight.

For the masala stuffing

Boil the yam and colocasia separately and set aside. Heat oil in a pan and add the sliced onion, ginger and green chilli, frying for a few minutes.

Add the cooked yam and colocasia, put the lid on the pan and cook for a few minutes. Add the mashed potato and season with salt.

To make the herb dosa

Heat a griddle to a high temperature and add a little ghee or oil.

Spread the dosa batter in a circular shape on the griddle with a small steel bowl and pour a little oil on top.

Once it has turned to a light brown colour, spread the stuffing on top and roll it from side to side.

Serve immediately with gooseberry chutney and apple chutney.

Larder THAN LIFE

The Larder on Goosegate is the elegant Hockley restaurant specialising in modern British favourites.

It's surely one of the most beautiful dining rooms in Nottingham with its original Victorian floor-to-ceiling windows overlooking the city's effortlessly trendy Hockley district.

And this uniquely lovely Grade II listed building also comes complete with an impressive history as the first ever apothecary of the one and only Jesse Boot, the Nottingham entrepreneur who founded the world famous retail chain.

Remnants of a fascinating past are still visible in the building's current incarnation as top restaurant The Larder on Goosegate, from original Victorian glass bottles on the dining tables to an imposing Boots sign which takes centre stage on the wall.

But history is by no means the main draw here. For the venue has rightly earned itself a reputation for superb food, with commendations in the Michelin Guide, the Good Food Guide and Harden's.

Opened in 2006, the Larder has been owned by journalist turned chef Ewan McFarlane since 2009 – with a menu offering simple but tasty classics based on a staple of modern British favourites.

Provenance of ingredients and sound cooking techniques form the basis of the laid back operation, led by head chef David Sneddon and front of house manager Anna Blachnia.

Signature dishes include a host of unusual cuts of steak, such as uniquely tender spider steaks and Pichana, an option not usually found in Britain but considered amongst the finest cuts of beef in places such as South America.

The à la carte menu contains a selection of other mouthwatering choices, with starters such as goat's cheese, pork, ox tongue, haggis and house cured salmon.

Mains include sea bass, lemon sole, lamb rump and Loomswood Farm duck breast, while exquisite puddings such as apple amber tart or roasted white chocolate mousse provide another highlight at this relaxed and inviting eatery.

The Larder on Goosegate

Boots
CASH CHEMISTS

Carefully prepared from
the purest ingredients by
Boots
CASH CHEMISTS

Boots Ca

The Larder's Savoury Cheesecake
WITH COLWICK CHEESE HERITAGE BEETROOT & COBNUTS

This is one of the Larder's most popular starters, with truly local ingredients – we buy our heritage beetroot and cobnuts from the Fruit Basket in West Bridgford. You will need four metal rings (usually sold as 'mousse rings') approximately 3cm tall and 7cm across. Serves four.

Ingredients

280g Colwick cheese

100g cream cheese

110g double cream

1 tablespoon blue poppy seeds

65g oatcakes

30g unsalted butter

Roasted beetroot – one each golden, candystripe, Chioggia, purple beetroot

Beetroot purée made from one large purple beetroot, 50g sugar, 50g white wine vinegar

Hazelnut dressing made from 3 tablespoons hazelnut oil, 1 tablespoon white wine vinegar, plus seasoning to taste

Handful of cobnuts or hazelnuts, lightly toasted

Salad leaves for garnish

Method

Make the cheesecake base by crushing the oatcakes and combining in a pan with the melted butter.

Once slightly cooled, divide into four and press into the base of the metal rings on a tray or plate, place in fridge to set.

To make the cheesecake mix, gently warm the cream, then place all of the ingredients in a blender and pulse until combined. Again, divide into four and spoon onto the set bases. Refrigerate for at least three hours.

Meanwhile, wrap all the beetroot individually in foil and roast in a medium oven for approximately 90 minutes or until tender (a sharp knife should go through to the centre with no resistance).

Once cooked, unwrap and remove the skin which should rub away easily.

Set aside the beetroot for the purée and dice the remaining roast beetroot to approximately 1cm square.

In a food processor, add the beetroot for puréeing (roughly chopped) with the sugar and vinegar. Blend until smooth, adjusting seasoning to taste.

Combine the ingredients for the dressing by whisking to emulsify.

To finish, remove the cheesecakes from the rings. Use either a thin-bladed knife to remove the cheesecake, or a blowtorch to gently warm the outside of the mould.

Place in the centre of a plate or bowl.

Dress the roasted beetroot and salad leaves with the hazelnut dressing and arrange around the cheesecake with the toasted cobnuts.

Spoon over the beetroot purée and serve.

Acclaim, awards and AUTHENTICITY

Since taking on the ownership of premier Indian restaurant MemSaab in 2012, Amita Sawhney has continued a success story which has seen the business win widespread acclaim and numerous prestigious awards.

Authentic Indian food coupled with an unrivalled fine dining experience are the ingredients that make MemSaab a restaurant in a league of its own in Nottingham.

Perfectly spiced curries, delicious barbecued meats, delicately flavoured seafood and superb desserts are amongst the mouthwatering highlights – with imaginative and beautifully presented dishes showcasing the very best in modern Indian cooking.

Established in 2002, the Maid Marian Way venue is now owned by Amita Sawhney, who comes from a family steeped in the restaurant business.

The Observer said MemSaab serves "amongst the top five curries in the country," while Harden's UK Restaurant Guide said it was "a class above other Nottingham Indians."

The Rough Guide called MemSaab "one of a new breed of Indian restaurants with crisp modern décor and bags of space – the food is quite exquisite."

Meanwhile, none other than food critic AA Gill, of The Sunday Times, said in March 2014: "MemSaab Nottingham is amongst the top three Indian restaurants in the country."

Featured in the Michelin Guide 2014, 2013, 2012 and 2011, the restaurant was this year named Nottingham's Best Independent Business and won the Nottingham Post's Indian Restaurant of the Year Award 2013.

It has also been runner up in the Observer Food Monthly Awards in 2014, 2013, 2012 and 2011, having previously been named Best Indian in the Nottingham Restaurant Awards in 2008, 2007, 2006 and 2005.

From its sumptuous, glittering interior to the friendly and professional team of staff, it's the attention to detail that makes a visit to MemSaab such a memorable experience.

The spacious but refined and elegant restaurant comfortably seats 200 diners and also has two private dining rooms, with a combination of traditional craftsmanship and vibrant modern art capturing the true essence of India's past and present.

The menu is packed with fine dining surprises, such as beautifully cooked fillet steak or delicately spiced salmon tikka – all served up in a reassuringly relaxed setting.

The top team of chefs have a strong knowledge of regional dishes from India and Pakistan – each offering their own individual interpretation to create modern classics.

Thanks to Amita's influence, MemSaab has fully embraced the best in modern Indian cuisine, with tempting and exciting choices such as John Dory with peas, soft shell crab, and beef steak with a chilli, coconut or saffron sauce.

Amita is proud to take on the position as the face of this thriving venue, with a warm smile and a cheery welcome for all her customers.

She remains on hand each evening to suggest dishes cooked and spiced according to the diner's particular taste – and she knows how to make a simple meal with friends and loved ones a real occasion.

It's no wonder MemSaab attracts illustrious visitors such as world renowned Indian chef Atul Kochhar – who was recently a special guest as part of a glittering charity evening where Amita raised over £20,000 for some great causes. This takes the total amount raised, over the years, to over £120,000!

In addition to Amita's Annual Charity Evening, MemSaab holds various events through the year including Wine and Food Pairing Evenings and Champagne and Food Pairing Evenings. MemSaab is the only Indian Restaurant in the region to host a Diwali Festival Week with Indian Street Food, Live Cooking Counters and lots of colour and sparkle!

Think you know Nottingham's legendary curry scene? Until you've been to MemSaab, you've only tasted half the story.

MemSaab's
LAHORI LAMB CHOPS

Try these tender marinated lamb chops, which go perfectly with a salad
and mint chutney dip. Serves four.

Ingredients

12 lamb chops

½ teaspoon clove powder

½ teaspoon garam masala

1 teaspoon red chilli powder

½ teaspoon salt

1 teaspoon tandoori paste

2 tablespoons vegetable or cooking oil

2 teaspoons ginger garlic paste

2 tablespoons lemon juice

1 tablespoon yoghurt

2 tablespoons mashed papaya, to
tenderise the meat

Method

In a large bowl mix all the ingredients (excluding the chops) into a paste. This can be done using a large spoon.

When the paste is ready, add 12 lamb chops, stir in, cover and marinate in the fridge for 24 hours.

When you are ready to cook, pop them onto the BBQ or grill under a high heat. Turn over after a few minutes and cook the other side.

Serves immediately and enjoy!

Digging up a
SUNDAY FEAST

The Moleface Pub Company has got Nottingham covered when it comes to brilliant British food – with four atmospheric pubs offering top quality fare.

Classic British food using the finest ingredients served simply in a relaxed setting – that's what John Molnar has created with his award-winning Moleface pub group.

The Wollaton, Larwood & Voce in West Bridgford, The Lord Nelson in Burton Joyce and the Royal Oak in Radcliffe-on-Trent all have their own distinct identity – but they're united by a common mission to provide quality, old-fashioned meals.

It's a business that started nearly eight years ago when chef John decided he wanted to open his own place, which would be "somewhere you could get a really great Sunday roast."

Larwood & Voce came first, with John sourcing much of his fruit and veg from local allotments, and the formula was an immediate winner. Within a year, he'd nabbed the Best Pub Food accolade at the Nottingham Restaurant Awards as well as being featured in the Good Food Guide.

After just 12 months, the Lord Nelson opened, followed by The Wollaton and the Royal Oak – with many from the original team still with John all these years later, including trusty executive chef Leroy.

Moleface provide a high quality twist on old British favourites, with superb fare such as steak and oyster pudding, game, Scotch eggs, fresh fish and chips and cheese from Colston Bassett. And of course, there's that sumptuous Sunday roast, including to-die-for Yorkshire Puddings and big fat roast potatoes cooked in beef dripping.

John reckons his staff are serving up about 800 roast dinners every Sunday. His philosophy is that everyone should truly feast on this special day or, as he puts it, "have to undo a belt knot or two."

The team has even created its own sauce range – try the outstanding "proper horseradish" for size.

The pubs also make their own bread and create gorgeous homemade cakes and nostalgic sweets like treacle sponge, sticky toffee pudding, and jam roly poly to transport you straight back to the good old days.

The Moleface Pub Co.

the lord 'nelson
pub & kitchen

thelordnelson

best food offer for
top 150 independent
retailers

2010, 2011, 2012, 2013

Observer Food Monthly
awards
-best Sunday lunch

HARVEST PALE

SHARP'S DOOM BAR

pizzas
emade ice creams
ottled beers
soft drinks

elson's

Moleface's
CLASSIC PRAWN COCKTAIL

This time-honoured starter is the perfect way to kick off your Sunday lunch. Buy the best quality prawns you can get your hands on or go for cooked and peeled ones from a fishmonger, remember the fresher the better. Serves four.

Ingredients

1 iceberg lettuce

400g fresh peeled prawns, cooked

1 lemon, quartered

Half a loaf brown bread

Butter for spreading

Smoked paprika

For the Marie Rose sauce:

100g mayonnaise

50g tomato sauce

1 tablespoon brandy

1 tablespoon Worcester sauce

2 splashes Tabasco

1 teaspoon horseradish

Lemon juice to taste

Salt

White pepper

Method

First make the Marie Rose sauce by mixing all the ingredients together. Season with salt and white pepper and refrigerate.

Discard the outer leaves of the lettuce, quarter and remove the core, then slice as finely as possible. Place in your serving bowls.

Season the prawns with salt, white pepper and a pinch of smoked paprika.

Place on top of the lettuce, then smother with the Marie Rose sauce.

Serve with a wedge of lemon and a slice of buttered brown bread.

Moleface's
ENGLISH ROAST BEEF (AND FRIENDS)

The cornerstone of the British Sunday lunch. Moleface have bought the same beef from Richard Taylor for their Sundays since day one. Use a good quality prime cut like the fore rib, marbled with plenty of fat for moisture and flavour. This recipe serves eight.

Ingredients

For the beef and gravy

3kg fore rib of beef on the bone (Moleface prefer an English grass fed Galloway beef aged for at least four weeks)

1 tablespoon Coleman's English mustard powder

1 onion, halved

1 bulb of garlic, halved

3 carrots, halved

½ head celery, roughly chopped

1 leek, roughly chopped

20-30g plain flour (depending on how thick you like your gravy)

1 litre beef stock reduction

1 glass red wine

Maldon sea salt and pepper

For the Yorkshire puddings

Equal quantities of eggs, plain flour and full fat milk (make as much or as little as you fancy)

Vegetable oil

For the roast potatoes

2kg medium sized Maris Piper potatoes, peeled

200g beef dripping

10 cloves of garlic, bashed

1 bunch fresh thyme and rosemary

Maldon sea salt & pepper

Method

For the beef

Preheat the oven to 200°c.

Remove the beef from the fridge 30 minutes prior to cooking, and rub with the Maldon salt, pepper and mustard powder.

Place a large sturdy roasting pan in the oven to heat for five minutes, remove and place all of the vegetables in the pan.

Sit the beef on top and roast for around 1 hour 20 minutes for medium rare or leave for longer if you prefer it well done.

Baste occasionally with the juices from the pan.

Once cooked, remove the beef from the roasting pan and place on a carving board. Cover with a tea towel and leave to rest.

Back to the roasting pan, add the flour to the roasted vegetables, then pour in the red wine and stir until smooth. Add a ladle of beef stock to the pan one at a time, stirring until the sauce is smooth.

Gently simmer the gravy for ten minutes, then pass through a sieve into a gravy jug.

For the Yorkshire puddings

Preheat the oven to 200°c.

Crack the eggs into a bowl and whisk in the flour until smooth.

Gradually whisk in the milk until fully incorporated, pass through a sieve to remove any lumps (this is best done the night before).

Place a tablespoon of vegetable oil into each well of a deep Yorkshire pudding tray and heat in the oven for ten minutes.

Remove the tray from the oven and pour in the batter until you have half-filled each well.

Place the tray into the oven for 30 minutes. Remove and keep warm.

For the roast potatoes

Preheat the oven to 200°c.

Place the potatoes in a pan, cover with water, add salt and bring to the boil until the potatoes are around three quarters cooked.

Drain and toss to give the potatoes a nice ruffled exterior.

Put the potatoes into a roasting pan with the beef dripping, adding the garlic, thyme and rosemary.

Place in the oven and roast for about 45 minutes.

Moleface's
ENGLISH ROAST BEEF (AND FRIENDS)
CONTINUED...

Ingredients

For the cauliflower cheese

1 head of cauliflower, cored and broken into florets

20g unsalted butter

20g plain flour

250ml full fat milk

½ onion

6 cloves

1 bay leaf

50g mature Cheddar cheese

1 teaspoon English mustard

Maldon sea salt & pepper

For the carrots

8 whole carrots, peeled

2 tablespoons marmalade

1 tablespoon soft brown sugar

20g butter

Maldon sea salt

For the roast parsnips

6 parsnips, peeled quartered and cored

30ml rapeseed oil

30ml Wollaton honey

1 teaspoon chopped thyme leaves

Maldon sea salt and pepper

For the Savoy cabbage

1 Savoy cabbage, cored quartered and finely sliced

100g soft unsalted butter

50g chopped walnuts

Maldon sea salt & pepper

For the rainbow chard

3 heads rainbow chard, cut into one inch pieces

Maldon sea salt and pepper

20g unsalted butter

100ml chicken stock

Method

For the cauliflower cheese

Preheat the oven to 200°c.

Bring a pan of salted water to the boil and blanch the cauliflower for two minutes.

Drain and place into a baking dish.

In a saucepan, melt the butter and stir in the flour to make a roux. Cook on a very low heat for ten minutes, stirring occasionally.

Meanwhile, stud the onion with the bay leaf and cloves, place in a pan with the milk and bring to a boil.

Turn off the heat. Once cooked, add a ladle of milk to the roux one at a time stirring until smooth. Repeat until all the milk has been incorporated and you have a smooth silky sauce.

Add the cheese and mustard and check the seasoning.

Pour the sauce over the cauliflower and bake in the oven for 20-30 minutes.

For the carrots

Put the whole peeled carrots and all the other ingredients into a saucepan.

Cover with water and bring to a rapid boil, cooking until the carrots are tender and the liquid has reduced to a syrupy glaze.

For the parsnips

Preheat the oven to 200°c.

Place the parsnips into a roasting tin, cover with rapeseed oil and season.

Roast for 30 minutes, remove from the oven and pour on the honey and thyme, giving them a little shake.

Place back in the oven for a further five minutes until crisp and golden.

For the Savoy cabbage

First make the walnut butter by beating the butter until it is light and creamy.

Stir in the chopped walnuts and season, then roll in cling film and refrigerate.

Bring a pan of salted water to the boil and drop in the cabbage. Cook for two minutes, drain and place in a serving bowl.

Remove the cling film from the walnut butter, slice and place on top of the cabbage.

For the rainbow chard

In a frying pan, heat the butter with the chicken stock and drop in the chard.

Wilt and season with Maldon salt.

Lay up the dining table, get your family round and tuck into the best Sunday roast going!

The famous Moleface Sticky Toffee Pudding
WITH TOFFEE SAUCE AND CORNISH CLOTTED CREAM

One of the big hitters at Moleface pubs, this pudding has been on the menu from day one – a sublime classic. This recipe serves eight "proper" pudding portions.

Ingredients

175g butter

250g soft brown sugar

250g muscavado sugar

500g pitted dates

1 teaspoon bicarbonate of soda

1 breakfast tea bag

500g self raising flour

½ tablespoon baking powder

6 free-range eggs, beaten

250g Rodda's clotted cream

For the sauce

200g soft brown sugar

200g muscavado sugar

800ml double cream

75g unsalted butter

Method

For the pudding

Preheat the oven to 160˚c.

Place the dates, tea bag and bicarbonate of soda in a saucepan and cover with cold water.

Bring to a gentle simmer and occasionally stir until the prunes have absorbed the water and resemble a purée.

Cream together the butter and both of the sugars. Add the prune purée to the creamed butter and sugar.

Sieve in the self raising flour and baking powder, stirring until you have a smooth mixture.

Slowly stir in the beaten eggs until you have a nice smooth sticky toffee batter.

Pour into a greased baking tin and double cover with silver foil.

Bake for 45 minutes to one hour, until the pudding is firm to the touch.

For the sauce

Bring the double cream and both sugars to a gentle simmer for five minutes.

Remove from the heat and stir in the butter until it has all melted and you have a smooth shiny toffee sauce.

Turn out the pudding into a slightly larger baking tin, pour over the toffee sauce and place back in the oven on 130˚c, for another 5 minutes.

Remove from the oven and serve with a generous dollop of clotted cream.

Now loosen the belt, approach the sofa and snooze!

Smoked to PERFECTION

Perkins has been a highlight of Nottinghamshire's culinary scene since 1982 – specialising in rural food with a very modern approach.

When Dr Beeching in his great wisdom decided to shut down Plumtree Railway Station in the 1960s, few could have imagined the next phase of this historic site's journey.

After standing derelict for decades, it was in 1982 when Tony and Wendy Perkins decided to turn the old railway into a chic new bistro – and a legendary local restaurant name was born.

Perkins has been run by brothers Jonathan and David Perkins since 2002 and, alongside talented chef director Sarah Newham, they've built a thriving business combining the best in fresh local produce, a passionate kitchen and constant innovation.

Inspiring and ever-changing menus are the order of the day at this genuine Notts institution.

With more than 30 years of expertise behind them, the team has created a food offering built on seasonality, while the kitchen sources superb local produce to ensure the journey from farm to fork is made in the shortest time possible.

Ingredients here often benefit from the amazing Perkins smokehouse, one of the very few seen in any UK restaurant. Over the past few years, the venue has developed its own ingenious smoking techniques, with the likes of smoked salmon, mackerel, haddock, mushrooms and local cheeses among the truly unique fare available.

The excellent à la carte and prix fixe menus offer an array of exciting options created from the likes of Clipston on the Wolds beef, Tollerton pork, Vale of Belvoir lamb and game together with beautiful local vegetables from the surrounding fields. Regular events include Friday steak nights, brilliant Saturday breakfasts and exceptional Sunday lunches.

Of course, the beautifully restored Victorian railway setting is a wonderful high spot of any visit to Perkins. The fabulous building has been respectfully renovated to create an atmospheric, unique and effortlessly stylish eatery.

Whether you're here for a formal business lunch, an intimate dinner for two, afternoon tea or a group celebration, there are plenty of reasons to make Perkins your next stop on the line.

Perkins
HERITAGE SALAD

Serves two.

Ingredients

1 ruby carrot, cooked, peeled & sliced

1 golden carrot, cooked, peeled & sliced

1 satin carrot, cooked, peeled & sliced

1 cylindrical beetroot, cooked, peeled & sliced

2 radishes, cut in to thin slices

1 small frisee lettuce, picked and washed

Truffle oil

35g grated Parmesan

2 soft boiled quail eggs, halved

6 pieces pickled candied beetroot

6 pieces pickled golden beetroot

25ml vinaigrette and honey to sweeten

1 lemon, juice only

For the pickled beetroot

1 candied beetroot, peeled and sliced as thin as possible

1 golden beetroot, peeled and sliced as thin as possible

500ml white wine vinegar

125ml water

250g caster sugar

3 star anise

1 clove

1 cinnamon stick

1 tablespoon white peppercorns

½ tablespoon coriander seeds

½ tablespoon fennel seeds

For the balsamic roast cherry tomatoes

6 cherry tomatoes

Splash balsamic vinegar

Splash olive oil

Salt and pepper

For the truffle mayonnaise

½ pint vegetable oil

2 egg yolks

½ teaspoon Dijon mustard

1 teaspoon white wine vinegar

Lemon juice to taste

Truffle oil to taste

Ground white pepper

Salt

For the parsnip crisps

1 parsnip

Vegetable oil, for frying

Method

For the pickled beetroot

Place all the ingredients except the beetroots into a large pan. Bring to the boil, reduce the heat and simmer for 15 minutes. Remove from the heat, cover with cling film and leave until cold. Once cold, strain and keep the liquid in the fridge until needed.

To pickle the beetroots, place both beetroots in separate bowls, pour over enough of the pickling liquor to cover and leave for at least one hour before using. Be careful – if left for too long the beetroot will loose its colour.

For the balsamic roast cherry tomatoes

In a hot pan roast tomatoes in olive oil for approximately 30 seconds.

Deglaze the pan with balsamic vinegar, season with salt and pepper, leave to cool.

For the truffle mayonnaise

In a large bowl place the egg yolks, white wine vinegar and mustard.

Whisk the ingredients together, then slowly add the oil.

When all the oil is incorporated, season to taste with truffle oil, lemon juice, salt and pepper.

For the parsnip crisps

Peel the parsnips, discard the skin then keep peeling the parsnip to produce thin strips of parsnip.

Heat a deep fat fryer to 180°c.

In small batches fry the parsnips until golden brown.

Dry on paper towel, then season with salt.

To finish

Arrange ingredients on a plate.

We use our own honey and mustard dressing to dress the carrots (any quality vinaigrette will be suitable, ensure you add a small amount of honey to sweeten the taste)

In a bowl place the frisee, grated Parmesan and tablespoon of truffle mayonnaise, lightly bind the leaves and then place in the middle of the plate, along with the quail eggs.

Garnish with parsnip crisps.

Perkins Roast Venison Haunch

SMOKED BEETROOT, KOHLRABI PURÉE, FONDANT POTATO

Serves two.

Ingredients

2 pieces of trimmed venison, between 180-200g in weight

2 baking potatoes

1 whole kohlrabi

125g salted butter

1 pint milk, just enough to cover the kohlrabi

Sprigs of thyme

100g green beans, topped and tailed, blanched and refreshed

6 pieces smoked beetroot, if you don't have the means to smoke the beetroot, normal beetroot will be fine

1 parsnip

100ml red wine jus

Salt and pepper

3 cloves garlic

1 pint vegetable stock, just enough to reach the top of the potato

Method

For the fondant potato

Take two large baking potatoes and cut out a round fondant using a large metal ring as a guide, cut the top and bottom of the potato so it has two flat sides.

In a solid base pan add butter, vegetable stock, salt and pepper, garlic and sprigs of thyme. Place the potatoes into the pan on a high heat in the middle of the stove. Do not shake the pan!

Once the liquid has fully reduced the butter will turn the base of the potatoes a golden brown colour, at this point remove from the heat.

Carefully remove from the pan with a spatula and serve golden brown side facing upwards.

For the kohlrabi purée

Peel and cut kohlrabi into small cubes.

Place in a pan and cover with milk, bring to the boil then reduce to a simmer until soft.

When cooked strain the kohlrabi and keep the milk to one side.

Using a food processor blitz the kohlrabi, add a little of the milk to make the purée smooth then season with salt and pepper.

Pass the purée and keep warm until needed.

For the smoked beetroot

Peel two ruby beetroots and cut in to slices about 3mm thick.

Place in a tray and smoke for around 8 hours.

Remove from the smoke house and place in a tray, cover with a little vegetable stock and butter then braise in the oven at 180°c for around 10 minutes until soft, but still with a little bite.

When cooked leave on one side until needed.

To finish

Place the seasoned venison in a hot pan with a splash of olive oil and a sprig of thyme, seal on all sides.

Add a knob of butter to the pan, then place the venison in the preheated oven at 180°c and cook for around 4-5 minutes for medium rare (you can cook the venison for longer if you prefer your meat better cooked).

Remove the venison from the oven, leave to rest for 5 minutes.

While the venison is resting, get the other ingredients hot and ready to plate.

When the venison has rested, carve and plate up the dish.

It's all about what you're
PUDDING IN

The revived Trinity Square in Nottingham city centre is home to The Pudding Pantry, a scrumptiously creative coffee shop specialising in the sweetest of treats.

If you've ever fancied sticky toffee pudding or salted caramel brownies at 8am in the morning (and who hasn't?), Nottingham now has the perfect venue to satisfy your most decadent cravings.

The Pudding Pantry is a dessert-based eatery producing wonderful cakes, pastries and other sweet treats from scratch using the freshest local ingredients.

The quirky café opened in spring 2014 and has already created something of a buzz, with Jordan from the Great British Bake Off amongst a growing army of regulars.

It was founded by Anthony Quinn, who has spent more than 13 years working in hospitality and fine dining. He's joined here by friends Georgina Mak, a talented pastry chef, and Amy Fish, who has worked in the food and drink industry for nearly 15 years both as a chef and a barista.

Their insatiable desire to provide the kind of food and coffee that will keep customers coming back time and again is infectious. Nearly everything is made in-house, from the huge array of cakes, to the ice cream, custard, baked beans and ketchup.

Bread is supplied by local hero Baz from Nottingham-based Bake Off and Pie, using flour from Green's Windmill. The excellent coffee is sourced from Ozone, a superb roastery sharing the Pudding Pantry's passion for quality.

The client base ranges from students, families and OAPs to suited businessmen and professionals, all clamouring to sample marvellous breakfasts, brunches, lunches and the ever-changing specials menu.

The chefs keep an eye out for new foodie trends, coming up with new twists on old classics – such as yummy orange treacle tart served with thyme and honey roasted plums. The focus here is on good old-fashioned, no-nonsense indulgence.

With its welcoming atmosphere and rustic but contemporary décor, you'll always be in for a treat inside The Pudding Pantry.

No wonder the venue won the regional semi-finals of The Big Start Up Loans competition, travelling to London for the exclusive awards ceremony at the Lord Mayor's office.

The Pudding Pantry's carrot cake doughnuts
WITH CARAMELISED WALNUTS, ORANGE SYRUP AND WHITE CHOCOLATE AND CARDAMOM ICE CREAM

A naughty but nice classic, full of surprising flavour combinations. Serves eight.

Ingredients

For the doughnuts

250ml buttermilk, at room temperature

14g fresh yeast

1 large egg

1 large egg white

55g light brown sugar

130g coarsely grated carrot

500g plain flour

1 teaspoon ground cinnamon

1 teaspoon ground ginger

½ teaspoon salt

¼ teaspoon ground nutmeg

45g unsalted butter, room temperature

Vegetable oil, for frying

For the caramelised walnuts

200g walnut pieces, lightly toasted

100g caster sugar

30ml water

1 teaspoon lemon juice

For the orange syrup

115g caster sugar

Juice from 2 oranges

Zest from 1 orange

30ml water

For the white chocolate & cardamom ice cream

240g chopped white chocolate

250ml whole milk

500ml double cream

200g caster sugar

Pinch of salt

5 egg yolks

1 vanilla pod, seeds removed

1 tablespoon crushed cardamom pods

Method

For the doughnuts

Place all the ingredients into a bowl of an electric mixer fitted with a dough hook attachment, mix on low speed until blended.

Increase to a medium speed and knead for about four minutes until the dough is smooth and elastic.

You can also mix the ingredients by hand and turn out the dough onto an oiled surface and knead until smooth, it will take about seven minutes.

Place the dough in an oiled bowl and cover with cling film. Leave to prove in a warm place for about 90 minutes or until it has risen and doubled in size.

Turn out the dough onto an oiled surface and roll to ¾ inch thickness.

Cut the doughnuts using a round cutter and scoop out a hole from the middle using a smaller cutter.

Re-roll the scraps of dough and cut out doughnuts until you have none left. Place them on a greased baking tray.

Cover with a damp tea towel and prove for 30 minutes.

Preheat the vegetable oil to 180°c in a table top fryer, or in a deep pot filled with two inches of oil over a medium high heat.

Carefully place two or three doughnuts in, leaving enough space so they do not touch and cook for two minutes on each side until golden brown.

Lift the doughnuts out with a slotted spoon and place on a wire rack with a kitchen paper lined tray underneath to drain and cool.

For the caramelised walnuts

Bring the sugar, water and lemon juice to the boil in a medium saucepan over a high heat.

As the sugar boils, brush the sides of the pan with a pastry brush dipped in water.

The mixture will turn a golden amber colour.

Remove the pan from the heat and stir in the walnut pieces.

Quickly turn out the walnuts onto a greased baking tray and spread out with a silicone spatula to cool.

For the orange syrup

Combine all the ingredients into a small saucepan and boil until thickened.

For the white chocolate & cardamom ice cream

Place the chocolate in a large bowl with a fine mesh sieve over the top of the bowl.

In a medium saucepan, add the milk, cream, salt, cardamom pods and scraped out vanilla seeds and pod. Heat over a high heat until just under a boil.

Remove from the heat and allow 10-15 minutes for the flavours to infuse.

Using a large bowl, whisk the egg yolks and sugar until pale and fluffy.

Bring the liquid cream mixture back up to the boil, and spoon over a little of the egg mixture. Whisk together to warm the egg mixture up.

Pour the rest of the cream mixture over the egg mixture, stirring well.

Add the whole mixture back into the saucepan and cook over a medium heat, stirring constantly for five minutes, until it thickens and coats the back of a wooden spoon.

Pour this custard mixture through the sieve over the white chocolate. Stir the mixture until all the chocolate is melted.

Place the bowl in an ice bath, stirring occasionally until the mixture is cool. Cover and chill in the refrigerator for at least eight hours or overnight.

Freeze in an ice cream machine according to the manufacturer's instructions.

Tales from the RIVERBANK

With its wonderful setting on Trent Bridge, the Riverbank is an elegant bar and restaurant housed inside one of the city's best known buildings.

Exquisite food in a chic setting next to Victoria Embankment are the delicious ingredients that make a visit to the Riverbank Bar and Restaurant an essential Nottingham experience.

The 100-year-old pub building – variously known as Casa, the Aviary and the Town Arms – is a familiar local landmark, standing in a prominent position on busy Trent Bridge.

It had been derelict for several years before the team behind Tom Brown's Brasserie and the Farndon Boathouse decided to add it to their repertoire of quality Trentside eateries in 2010.

With its stunning riverside views and walks along the leafy Embankment, the pub has been extensively converted into a stylish and modern 250-capacity bar and 110-seater restaurant, featuring a separate gallery function room.

Outside, there's an extensive ultra-chic, all-weather terrace with wild-flame heaters and sunken wind-free enclaves to keep you snug and warm in winter – and it's perfectly shaded from the sun and showers during our glorious English summers.

The Riverbank's state-of-the-art, architect-designed bar and brasserie-style restaurant serves some of the best grub around under the creative supervision of head chef, Mark Osborne.

His kitchen ethos is to source the finest local produce to create simple and affordable, yet well-cooked tasty cuisine concentrating on a super choice of comfort food favourites.

Choose from a menu of traditional fish and chips, scrumptious gourmet burgers, succulent steaks, grills and salads, with plenty of daily specials and "cheffy dishes" on offer to tempt even the most discerning foodie.

This refined but very welcoming space is ideal whether you want to dine out in style or grab a quick bite with friends.

As the newest addition to a family-run business which opened its first venue in 1986, expect the Riverbank to continue serving up this sophisticated fare for many years to come.

The Riverbank's roast scallops
WITH ARTICHOKE PURÉE, ROAST PUMPKIN, PUMPKIN SEEDS AND GRANNY SMITH

Create the wow factor with this scrumptious seafood classic. Serves four.

Ingredients

12 large scallops

300g Jerusalem artichokes

1 small pumpkin

1 Granny Smith apple

50g butter

Olive oil

Sea salt

Five-spice powder

1 small cup of milk

½ lemon

Pepper

Method

For the artichoke purée

Peel the artichokes and place in a saucepan.

Top up with water to just cover and then add the cup of milk. Cook until soft and strain, saving back any leftover water.

Place in a blender and blitz until smooth, adding a little of the water if needed. Season to taste with salt and pepper.

For the roast pumpkin

Heat the oven to180°c.

Peel the pumpkin and dice into 1cm cubes, keeping the seeds.

Place in a baking tray and spoon over a little olive oil, seasoning with the five-spice powder.

Place in the oven for ten minutes and then add the pumpkin seeds.

Continue to cook for a further 10-15 minutes until soft and golden.

To serve

In a heavy non-stick frying pan, sauté the scallops for 30 seconds on either side or until they are lightly coloured.

Squeeze in the lemon juice and add a spoon of butter. Season and set aside.

Place a couple of spoonfuls of artichoke purée on the plates and top with the roast pumpkin.

Place on the scallops and sprinkle over the seeds.

Garnish with slices of Granny Smith apple.

Sam & Amy's
CHOCOLATE BROWNIE CUPCAKES

Sam Pinkham and Amy Voce are better known as Gem 106 breakfast show presenters Sam and Amy – and their lively approach has been waking up East Midlands folk for the past eight years.

The duo won Gold in the Music Personality of the Year category at the 2014 Radio Academy Awards, beating off the likes of Chris Evans, Graham Norton, Christian O'Connell and Mark Radcliffe.

Their amazing success has now led to the Nottingham-based pair being offered prestigious presenting roles at BBC Radio 2.

Sam admits to being useless in the kitchen but talented Amy is a keen baker and regularly blogs favourite recipes. This inventive brownie recipe is one of her favourites, especially the blow torch part. Makes twelve.

Ingredients

For the brownies

225g plain chocolate broken into pieces

85g butter

2 large eggs

200g soft dark brown sugar

1 teaspoon vanilla extract

140g plain flour

For the meringue

4 egg whites

225g sugar

30ml coffee liqueur

2 teaspoons espresso coffee

Blow torch (optional)

Method

For the brownies

Preheat the oven to 180°c.

Line a 12-hole muffin tin with 12 paper cases.

Place the chocolate and butter in a saucepan, heat gently, stirring constantly until melted. Remove from heat and stir until smooth. Leave to cool slightly.

Place the eggs and sugar in a large bowl and whisk together, then add the vanilla extract. Stir in the flour until combined, then stir in the melted chocolate until fully incorporated.

Spoon the mixture into the paper cases. Bake in the oven for 25 minutes, or until firm to the touch but still slightly moist in the centre.

Leave the cupcakes to cool for 10 minutes then transfer to a wire rack to cool completely.

For the meringue

Using an electric hand mixer, begin by beating four egg whites until they form stiff peaks. They should stand up straight when the whisk is removed.

Make a sugar syrup by mixing the sugar with six tablespoons of water. Stir the sugar and water together over a medium heat. Dip a pastry brush in water and brush any bits of sugar from the sides of the pan into the syrup to melt.

When all the sugar is dissolved, bring it to a fast boil until it reaches about 120°c.

As soon as the syrup reaches the correct temperature, pour onto the egg whites in a thin, steady stream as you whisk. Be careful not to pour the hot syrup directly onto the mixer beaters as it may stick or splash back at you.

Once the sugar is mixed, very slowly, making sure the meringue remains stiff, add the coffee liqueur and espresso coffee.

Continue to whisk the meringue until it has cooled. It should be shiny and stiff.

Spoon the meringue into a piping bag and pipe onto the brownies.

To add a more bronzed effect, finish off by lightly glazing the meringue with a blow torch. Enjoy!

Gastronomic DELIGHTS

The shadow of Clifton Boulevard is the unlikely setting for one of Britain's most incredible dining experiences, the two Michelin starred Restaurant Sat Bains with Rooms.

Awards, accolades and even two Michelin stars mean little to celebrated Nottingham chef Sat Bains – he's much more interested in his customers.

His passion for great food bursts out of every sentence he speaks, and his one goal at Restaurant Sat Bains with Rooms is to take customers on a thrilling culinary journey, giving them the best meal of their lives.

"Accolades and awards are fine, but they're not everything," he says. "Someone can walk into service tonight and it doesn't matter that I have two Michelin stars, I have nothing. It's a level playing field and we start from zero every time – it all depends on that night."

The stylish restaurant seats around 40 in an intimate, elegant and understated space where flavour is king. Sat and his highly skilled team of 36 staff are famed for their amazing seven-course or ten-course tasting menus with contrasting temperatures, tastes and textures taking diners through the full range of salt, sweet, sour, bitter and umami.

A typical "menu" might include scallop, smoked eel, aged beef, soft cheese, partridge, cheese, rice pudding, chocolate and blackberries. Everything here is fresh and seasonal, with exquisite dishes invented in the incredible development kitchen.

Sat has invested heavily in a new garden area where one of the UK's best growers is now in charge of superb produce for the restaurant. There's even a state-of-the-art composting machine, the only one of its kind in any restaurant in the country.

Yes, there are waiting lists to dine here and yes Sat has considered expanding. But he fears he would lose the special ambience he's created.

He's also keen that his restaurant should not just be a solemn shrine to gastronomy. He wants people to have a fun experience, where they can forget day-to-day worries and relax.

He explains: "I like the idea that people are laughing and being loud here. I like the women to be kicking their shoes off. Having the rooms is even better, because we see our customers again for breakfast and that makes the experience even better."

The goal here has always been to give people something they simply can't get anywhere else. Sat, alongside his wife Amanda, has ensured Nottingham is truly on the gastronomic map.

Pastry

Sat Bains' BEEF CHEEK AND OYSTERS

An amazing British dish, using tender braised beef cheek marinated in Shipstone's beer and honey for a bitter-sweet flavour. Serves four.

Ingredients

For the marinade

2 bottles of Shipstone's bitter
2 sprigs of thyme
2 sprigs of rosemary
10 juniper berries, crushed
8 cloves of garlic, crushed
50g honey
500ml Aspall's organic apple cyder vinegar

For the beef cheek

3kg beef cheek, silver skin and sinew removed and cut into 10 portions
500ml brown chicken stock
500ml white chicken stock

For the pickled shallots

1 large shallot, thinly sliced
50ml pickling juice

For the sea vegetables

20g sea purslane
20g rock samphire
20g stone crop

For the oyster emulsion

2 egg yolks
2 oysters, cooked
Squeeze of lemon juice
200ml parsley oil
Fine salt to taste

For the brown chicken stock

2kg chicken wings
1.5 litres sunflower oil
1kg unsalted butter
25g tomato purée

For the white chicken stock

2 whole chickens
2 shallots, chopped
4 sprigs of thyme

For the parsley oil

200g parsley
300ml sunflower oil
Pinch of salt

For the pickling juice

100g caster sugar
150ml white wine vinegar
You will also need wild garlic flowers

Method

For the marinade

Mix all the ingredients together and store in a container until needed.

For the beef cheek

Place the beef cheek in the marinade for 24 hours, drain and strain the liquid and pour it into a pressure cooker.

Reduce to a glossy syrup without the lid on.

Add the brown and white chicken stock and bring up to the boil. Take off the heat.

Heat a pan and sauté the beef cheek until brown all over. Add this to the pressure cooker along with any pan juices.

Bring up to full pressure and then turn down the heat a little and cook for 45 minutes.

Take off the heat and leave to cool in the pan. The cheek will be reheated in this later.

For the pickled shallots

Place the shallots in a sous vide bag and cover with some of the pickling juice.

Compress on full and leave in the bag until needed.

For the sea vegetables

Blanch the sea vegetables in boiling salted water. Refresh in ice cold water.

Strain through a colander and store in an airtight container until needed.

For the oyster emulsion

Place the egg yolks, oysters and lemon juice in a blender and blend on its lowest speed.

Once emulsified, slowly add the oil until it forms a mayonnaise-like consistency.

Pass the emulsion and check the seasoning. Store in an airtight container until needed.

For the brown chicken stock

Chop each wing into three pieces. Fill a deep-fat fryer with half sunflower oil and half butter. Bring to 120°c.

Add the wings and 'fry' until fully caramelised. This will take around 45 minutes.

Remove the wings and pat dry on kitchen towel. Place in a heavy-bottomed pan and cover with cold water.

Bring to a gentle simmer and add the tomato purée. Simmer for five hours, skimming off any scum throughout the cooking process.

Remove the bones and pass the stock through a fine mesh sieve. Leave to cool in the fridge overnight.

Remove any fat that has risen to the top and hardened. Bring the stock to the boil and rapidly reduce to the desired consistency.

Pass through a chinoise and store in the fridge until needed.

For the white chicken stock

Place the chickens, chopped shallots and thyme in a pressure cooker and cover with cold water.

Bring up to full pressure and cook for 25 minutes. Remove from the heat and allow to cool in the pressure cooker.

Strain through a fine mesh sieve. Leave to cool in the fridge overnight. Remove any fat that has risen to the top and hardened.

Strain the stock again and chill until needed.

For the parsley oil

Blanch the parsley in boiling salted water for one minute. Shock in iced water.

Pat the parsley dry, transfer to a blender, add the oil and blend on full power until smooth.

Place in a centrifuge and run on a 20 minute cycle with no heat. Strain off the vibrant, clear oil, leaving the sediment. Discard the solids.

Store in an airtight container for up to seven days.

For the pickling juice

Boil the sugar and vinegar for one minute until the sugar has dissolved.

Allow the juice to go cold. Pass through a chinoise. Store in an airtight container until needed.

Finishing the dish and presentation

We haven't put any emphasis on presentation because we want you to create your own interpretation of the dish. Alternatively you can follow the example shown here.

Spice Up Your LIFE

Sauce Shop is a fledgling Nottingham business with big ambitions to add more taste to the humble dinner table.

Keen amateur cooks Pam and James Digva have always liked to experiment with their food – and now their passion for great ingredients has turned from a hobby to a proper brand.

Sauce Shop, the West Bridgford couple's colourful range of sweet and savoury ketchups and table sauces, is now available at nine retailers and has wowed the crowds at big events such as the East Midlands Chilli Festival.

Established in February 2014, the idea was born after James cooked his own smoky chipotle ketchup which proved a real hit with friends and family.

He started making a few more sauces and the couple decided to take some along to West Bridgford Farmer's Market, with some hastily produced Dymo labels (still their cute branding quirk to this day). The range was a big local hit and Sauce Shop became a regular fixture at the market.

Pam and James buy all their fruit and veg from West Bridgford. The product is still handmade in small batches in their home kitchen, with no added water, no stabilisers and definitely no non-authentic substitutes such as onion powder or garlic powder. Their philosophy is "nothing bad put in, nothing good taken out."

There are currently ten rainbow coloured products in Sauce Shop's range – including delicious sweet, savoury, ketchups and chilli-based recipes. Their hero product is Nottinghamshire Sauce, the couple's own answer to HP sauce, which was famously invented here.

Nottinghamshire Sauce is mushroom-based with woody and earthy overtones, great with meat and, according to Pam and James, the perfect alternative to brown sauce.

All the sauces can be used both as an ingredient in favourite recipes, as a marinade or as a simple table sauce.

Look out for great new flavours coming soon, including scrumptious chocolate fudge.

The endlessly versatile
SAUCE SHOP COLLECTION

Pam and James have come up with some brilliant ideas for each of their Sauce Shop products – try these lip-smacking suggestions for size.

Nottinghamshire Sauce

Perfect with anything meaty, including cooked breakfasts, sausages and steak. Add to stews and casseroles for an extra savoury flavour.

Smoky Chipotle Ketchup

Great as a marinade for barbecued meats. A smoky accompaniment to ribs, chicken or potato wedges. Mix with mayonnaise to make a delicious dip or burger sauce.

Caramelised Onion Ketchup

Lightly spiced and oniony, this is an interesting alternative to tomato ketchup and totally completes a sausage sandwich. Use as a pizza topping or put it with a pie.

Tomato Ketchup

Sauce Shop ketchup is made using fresh vine ripened tomatoes – you might even see the odd seed in there. Perfect with chips, burgers and so much more.

Lime and Coriander Sauce

A favourite amongst Pam and James' friends, this is a lovely cooling accompaniment to nachos, chilli and curry. People also love it with fish and chicken.

Fiery Chilli Sauce

A great alternative to a fresh chopped red chilli, with just the right amount of heat and sweetness. Livens up stir-fries, curries and pasta dishes.

Buffalo Hot Sauce

The perfect pairing with fried chicken – smother loads of wings with sauce when they're still hot and serve with fries and slaw.

Really Hot Sauce

A little of this goes a long way. This is Sauce Shop's hottest sauce, but the fruity flavour of the Scotch Bonnet chilli makes it perfect for REAL chilli enthusiasts. Add to anything that needs a kick – even add a drop to cooking to spice things up.

Salted Caramel Sauce

Place spoon in bottle, eat sauce from spoon, that's what most people seem to do. However, you can also pour onto warm brownies, cheesecake, pancakes, waffles and ice cream. Or use as a baking ingredient – it creates an amazing toffee if baked in the oven.

Peanut Butter Sauce

A delicious dessert sauce for peanut butter fans. Perfect on ice cream, popcorn and cakes.

A taste of the
OLD COUNTRY

Savai have been serving up authentic Italian food in Nottingham since 1998.

Savai restaurant opened 16 years ago and was the first authentic Italian stone baked pizzeria in Nottingham, and the first outside of London. A novelty for the Midlands, Savai had a bustling business from the word go. It is a friendly, family run restaurant by brothers Mick and Tony, with a vibrant yet relaxed atmosphere where knowledgeable and personable staff cater for each individual.

Situated around the corner from the historic Lace Market as well as the Capital FM Arena and BBC studios, Savai has a buzz and ambience like no other.

The food is inspired by Italy, with many of the recipes taken from their family's restaurant of the same name in Campo San Martino in Padova. Over the years the menu has developed to include pasta dishes, steaks and grills as well as fish.

Throughout the years Savai has stood the test of time and remained open despite the recession and rising competition. They are proud to welcome customers who have dined with them since day one, and who are now bringing the next generation of family with them. Why? Their ethos is simple: they use fresh, fine ingredients to create quality dishes that are bursting with flavour. The dough is homemade, the meat is sourced locally from Owen Taylors and the fish from Westport Foods. Most other items are made from scratch in-house.

Savai's first recipe is a classic Penne Pugliese, which is very typical of the Puglia region. Here, the ingredients of olives, garlic, peppers and red onions are found in abundance. The spicy sausage is also very typical of the area as years ago the lack of wealth in southern communities meant they had to cure their meat in order for it to stay fresh. It has since remained a popular kind of delicacy.

The second recipe is a 'surf 'n' turf' style dish, a favourite of regular patron Carl Froch. Savai often get a few famous faces in through the doors, and Carl has since become a good friend of Mick and Tony's.

Savai

Savai's
PENNE PUGLIESE

This dish comes from the Puglia region of Italy, famed for their olive oil, peppers, tomatoes and spicy cured sausage. Serves four.

Ingredients

900ml passata (blended good quality plum tomato)

3 small mixed peppers, cut into small pieces. Once cut allow one hand of mixed peppers per person

1 small red onion, chopped

½ small white onion, sliced and chopped

1 teaspoon dried oregano

3 cloves garlic, finely chopped and crushed

3 teaspoons salt

Pinch ground black pepper

500g dried penne pasta

6 tablespoons virgin olive oil

200g Italian cured, spicy sausage or chorizo, cut into small bite-sized pieces

1 chicken or vegetable stock cube

1 tablespoon white granulated sugar

1 tablespoon tomato purée

2 tablespoons white wine

125ml water

To garnish

1 small bunch of basil or parsley, chopped

50g pecorino or Parmesan shavings

Method

For the tomato sauce

Sauté the white onion with 3 tablespoons of olive oil until soft in a pan. Add the garlic and cook gently for approximately 1 minute, but do not burn the garlic. Add the white wine and cook for 1 minute.

Add the passata to the pan and bring to the boil. Season with salt and pepper.

Add sugar, tomato purée, oregano and the crumbled stock cube. Add 125ml water and simmer for 20 minutes.

Adjust seasoning to taste.

For the Pugliese sauce

Whilst the tomato sauce is simmering add the penne into a pan of boiling salted water and cook accordingly.

In a separate large pan add 2 tablespoons of olive oil. Add the peppers and cook until softened.

Once the pasta is cooked place peppers, red onion and sausage with 2 tablespoons of olive oil to a large pan and cook for 3 minutes on a low-to-medium heat.

Once this is done add approximately 4 large ladles of prepared tomato sauce to the pan. Bring to the boil and add the pasta. Stir the pasta well and add 1 tablespoon olive oil until glossy. Add more sauce if necessary.

Place the finished pasta into individual pasta bowls adding remaining sauce if required.

Garnish with cheese and basil or parsley.

For a more spicy flavour, include chilli to your taste.

Carl Froch's
SAVAI STEAK & SEA BASS

Nottingham boxer Carl Froch is a four-time world champion in the super middleweight division, a Commonwealth title holder, and has been voted the best British pound-for-pound boxer according to the BBC, as well ranking as the number 8, pound-for-pound fighter in the world by BoxRec and The Ring magazine. Although a frequent jet-setter for international fights, Carl is no stranger to Savai after meeting Mick and Tony, the owners, a few years ago.

He's a regular face, affirming "aside from the fact that we're good friends, I go in there so often because the food is second to none."

This spicy steak and sea bass is a favourite of Carl's as it packs a punch and is always prepared according to his specific dietary requirements, which are strict when he's in training. This dish is perfect as it is high in protein and low in carbs.

The steak is delicious cooked medium rare and drizzled with chilli oil, with the fish dressed in garlic and chilli. For Carl this is simply served with broccoli or spinach, although you can add fries if you'd like to. Serves one hungry cobra!

Ingredients

8oz Owen Taylor prime English fillet steak

2 teaspoons sea salt

1 teaspoon coarse black pepper

10 teaspoons virgin olive oil

2 4oz sea bass skin on, bones removed

10g salted butter

2 cloves garlic, crushed

1 whole lemon

1 head broccoli

1 small bunch parsley, chopped

Fresh chillies, marinated in virgin olive oil

Method

Firstly cut the 8oz steak to make two even 4oz steaks.

Drizzle approximately 2 teaspoons of olive oil on the meat, then season with 1 teaspoon of sea salt and black pepper.

To make the dressing, mix the butter, 4 teaspoons of olive oil, lemon juices, half the crushed garlic, and 1 teaspoon of black pepper and 1 teaspoon of sea salt together. If it is too thick, squeeze in more lemon juice, so the dressing can be drizzled. Prepare the sea bass by coating the fish with half of the dressing.

Place the steak on a very hot grill pan or chargrill, and cook to your liking. Garnish by brushing some olive oil and parsley over.

Pour 4 teaspoons of olive oil onto a non stick frying pan over medium heat. Add the sea bass skin side down into the pan and cook for 2 minutes. Drizzle the remaining fish dressing on the sea bass and place the pan under a hot grill. Cook for a further 3 minutes. Place the sea bass on the plate and pour the juices from the pan as a garnish with some sea salt and parsley.

Cut the broccoli into florets and place into a pan of boiling salted water and cook for approximately 5 minutes. Whilst cooking the broccoli, heat 2 teaspoons of olive oil in a medium sized frying pan and add the remaining crushed garlic to the pan and cook for about 30 seconds, without burning the garlic. Drain the broccoli and place them into the pan with the garlic. Toss the florets, season to taste and serve with the steak and sea bass immediately. Use the fresh hot chillies and oil as a side-dip.

Brewing up a STORM

A beer which was first brewed in Nottingham in 1852 has been brought back to life with the relaunch of Shipstone's.

It's one of Nottingham's most famous brand names with a heritage stretching back more than 160 years – and now beer lovers are once again raising a glass to Shipstone's.

James Shipstone and Sons was run by the same family for four generations at the famous Star Brewery in Basford before the company was sold to Greenall's in 1978 and then sadly closed down in 1990.

One of a number of legendary Nottingham beers, the Shippo's name was so iconic that its heritage was worth handing down. Thanks to brewing industry professional Richard Neale and former Shipstone's brewer Colin Brown, the brand was reborn in 2013 amidst much local celebration.

After months spent tracking down original malt and hop ledgers and tracing the essential ingredients which made Shipstone's so popular, they were finally able to produce a hand crafted beer that tasted suitably great – and it's gone down a storm.

With orders from pubs all over the country, there are currently two beers in the range.

Shipstone's Original Bitter, available in cask and bottles, is brewed using the finest Marris Otter Malt and has a dry, clean and refreshing taste – perfect with grilled or roast meats. Meanwhile, the new cask-only Gold Star Blonde Ale is a smooth pale ale with a good balance of flavours and a light subtle hop finish. Try it with chicken, salads or even a curry.

Old blue eyes
IS BACK

Sinatra in Nottingham is a restaurant singing a brand new tune these days, with a brilliant refreshed menu and a sophisticated but fun vibe.

It's been a mainstay of the Nottingham social scene since 1995, but Sinatra in Chapel Bar has undergone something of a reinvention over the past 12 months.

Under the guidance of new owner Simon Patterson, the venue has had a complete refit, with smart modern décor, stripped floors and a funkier, fresher feel – including eye-catching lighting and beautiful modern furniture.

Simon, who previously ran favourite East Midlands hang-outs Fat Cat and BLUU, stepped in when the original much-loved but slightly tired Sinatra's went into administration in 2013.

Cleverly, he kept the name (albeit with the loss of an apostrophe) and with a few simple tweaks has created a reinvigorated mood – attracting a new largely 20-something clientèle thanks to a cracking cocktail selection and regular fun events such as Ladies Night.

And yes, those famous signed photos which once adorned the walls have gone – mostly sold at auction with a donation going to Ward E38 at the QMC in memory of the late Rosie Whittle, a friend of the family.

Most significantly, Simon has also streamlined the menu here – with a smaller choice of dishes but a major increase in quality. The emphasis is very much on European staples and you can choose from delicious pasta, fresh fish and pigeon alongside familiar old favourites such as the Sinatra burger.

With the average dish costing a great-value £9 and various pre-theatre offers, plus skilled and efficient service headed by chef Ryan Taylor, the rebirth has already proved a triumph.

The large outdoor seating area has helped transform Chapel Bar into a lovely al-fresco meeting place straight out of a French movie. No wonder the tables were packed throughout the unusually warm summer.

An ideal spot for business lunches and yummy mummys alike (check out the wonderful new children's menu), it's clear that Nottingham's own Sinatra will be in great voice for some time to come.

Sinatra's Parma Ham
WRAPPED MONKFISH FILLET

A deliciously summery main, usually served in the restaurant with parsley crushed new potatoes, sage creamed cabbage, carrot and celeriac infused with lemon and grain mustard. Serves one.

Ingredients

1 piece of monkfish fillet (180g)

2 slices of Parma ham

1 carrot

100g celeriac

100g Savoy cabbage, sliced

½ small onion

¼ leek

6 sage leaves, finely chopped

Zest of half a lemon

Juice of a quarter of a lemon

50ml white wine

200ml double cream

1 teaspoon wholegrain mustard

Pinch of salt and pepper

6-7 new potatoes

25g butter

25g parsley, finely chopped

Method

Prepare the fish by wrapping with two slices of Parma ham and rolling in cling film. Wrap tightly to hold the shape.

Dice the carrot and celeriac and simmer in seasoned water for 5 minutes. Add the sliced cabbage and cook for a further 2 minutes, then drain off the water.

In the same pan, fry the onion, leek, sage and lemon zest to soften. Add the wholegrain mustard, white wine and double cream. Cook for 10 minutes.

Unwrap the monkfish and pan fry to colour, then place in an oven at 220°c for 5-7 minutes.

Arrange on the plate with the sage creamed cabbage, adding crushed new potatoes mixed with butter and parsley.

Stuart Pearce

MY MUM'S CORNED BEEF PASTA

Nottingham Forest legend Stuart Pearce is a big fan of Italian food and here he showcases an old family dish.

This is something my mum used to make for me, my two brothers and sister when we were kids and I still love it now because it's so quick but really tasty. When we were kids you had no option but to eat what was put in front of you – you definitely couldn't say 'I don't like that.'

As well as Italian food, Stuart is also a fan of the traditional English roast. So is he a bit of a foodie?

"Well if you mean, do I like eating food? Then yes. But I need to leave feeling like I've been filled up. I'm not too sure about this arty stuff with small portions!"

This dish takes just 10-15 minutes to make. Serves two.

Ingredients

1 large onion, finely diced

Mushrooms (optional)

3 tablespoons tomato purée

1 large knob butter

1 large handful of a flavoursome cheese (preferably cheddar), grated

250g dried spaghetti

1 tin of finest corned beef

Salt & pepper for seasoning

Method

Place the spaghetti in a large pan of boiling water and while that comes to temperature, soften the onion by frying in a pan with the knob of butter.

If using mushrooms, add these to the onions after a few minutes, although I prefer to leave them out.

Trim the excess fat off the corned beef, then cut it into cubes. Add it to the onions, followed by the tomato purée and season with a little salt and plenty of black pepper.

Add a dash of the spaghetti cooking liquid to the frying pan to add a little more moisture.

Mix together and heat through on a low/medium heat.

To serve

Once the spaghetti is ready, drain the water and mix in with the sauce.

Top with cheese and serve.

We all scream
FOR ICE CREAM

Thaymar is the famous Notts name synonymous with delicious and unusual ice creams and sorbets – but there is so much more to this sweet family business.

Thaymar ice creams and fruit sorbets have provided the sweet smell of success for Haughton Park Farm near Bothamsall in Retford since 1988.

Thelma Cheetham and her late husband Martin stumbled upon their tasty business plan at a time when the introduction of new quotas in Britain meant they were producing way too much milk.

The clever couple diversified and devised a range of gorgeous and unusual ice cream combinations, using quality local fruit and natural flavours.

More than a quarter of a century later, Thaymar products are stocked nationwide and a thriving farm shop and tea room provide the ideal companion to the ice cream venture.

Thelma recalls the company started at a time when it really was rare for a food business to strike it rich. But people soon warmed to this coolest of collections, perhaps because of the heavy emphasis on local produce, with delicious ingredients like raspberries, elderflower and gooseberries sourced from neighbouring farms.

Thelma's children Emily and Thomas now help run the business, while it was elder son Christopher who had the idea to transform the old dairy into a cosy tea room. Despite very little advertising, scores of people take the turn off the A1 to discover the amazing treats in store every day.

Thaymar produces some 1,200 litres of ice cream a day, including surprising flavour ideas like Bakewell tart and lemon meringue. There are more than 35 speciality ice creams, sorbets and frozen yoghurts, with a 'just for adults' range including brandy and orange, Gaelic coffee and gin and tonic sorbet.

The fabulous shop stocks the farm's own beef and lamb, including pedigree short horn cattle and Hampshire Down sheep. And the ingredients used in the tea room are all for sale in the shop – so you can literally take the menu home with you.

The shelves here are bursting with specialist cheeses, sausages, bacon, smoked salmon, jams, dressing, chutneys, cakes and biscuits – and many popular tea room specials such as lamb tagine and chicken in Stilton are also available as the ultimate in ready meals.

Rocky Mountain
Honeycombe Ice Cream With
Chocolate, Nuts & Fudge
Allergy advice: Contains Milk, Soya & Nuts

Thaymar's Chicken
IN STILTON, APRICOTS AND MUSHROOMS

A wholesome and great tasting dish that's simple to prepare
but packed with personality. Serves four.

Ingredients

5 chicken breasts

1 large onion

400ml double cream

500ml chicken stock

1 tin apricot halves

150g closed cup white mushrooms

150g mature blue Stilton

1 tablespoon cornflour mixed with 1
tablespoon cold water to make a paste

Vegetable oil

Salt & pepper

Method

Finely dice the onion and sauté in a little oil until soft. Add the mushrooms and continue to fry for five minutes.

Lay the chicken breasts in a baking dish and cover with the stock. Bake in the oven at 190°c, for 25-30 minutes until the juices run clear.

Drain the juice from the apricots and add three tablespoons into the onions. Chop the apricot halves into three.

Add the apricots, Stilton and cream to the soft onions and cook through until the cheese has melted.

When the chicken is cooked, add the stock to the sauce.

Thicken with cornflour paste, bubble and season with salt and black pepper.

Pour the sauce over the chicken, crumble with a little more stilton and return to the oven until golden and bubbling.

Served with steamed greens.

Thaymar's Coconut and Raspberry Cake
WITH RASPBERRY AND WHITE CHOCOLATE TOPPING

A divine traditional cake infused with richly exotic flavours. Serves ten.

Ingredients

For the cake

100g coconut

250ml milk

200g butter

4 eggs

400g self raising flour

400g golden granulated sugar

100g fresh or frozen raspberries

For the icing

4 tablespoons raspberry coulis

300g icing sugar

65g butter

For the white chocolate topping

50g white chocolate

2 tablespoons double cream

Method

To make the cake

Soak coconut and milk together in a bowl for a minimum 2 hours or preferably overnight.

Preheat oven to 180°c.

Grease and line a 20x30x5cm cake tin with baking parchment.

In a large bowl cream the butter and sugar together then gradually add the beaten eggs.

Fold in the flour and soaked coconut.

Pour the mixture into the cake tin and level into the corners.

Drop the raspberries evenly on to the top of the cake mixture.

Bake 40-50 minutes until risen and firm.

To make the icing

Melt the butter and combine with the icing sugar and raspberry coulis.

Spread evenly on top of the cooled cake.

Finally, in a bowl over some hot water, melt the white chocolate and cream.

Drizzle onto the iced cake.

Serve cut into squares with a scoop of Thaymar coconut ice cream and a drizzle of raspberry coulis.

Quintessentially ENGLISH

Former interior designer Carolyn Cavell always dreamed of opening a quintessentially English tea room. And in May 2012, her vision became a sparkling reality with the opening of the supremely elegant Thea Caffea at Low Pavement.

With an abundance of big coffee chains springing up all over Nottingham since the new Millennium, tea devotee Carolyn Cavell felt the city was seriously lacking when it came to getting a decent cuppa.

Originally from the North East, she'd previously worked as an occupational therapist and later as an interior designer for her husband's property development business – which is when she became aware of a largely derelict building hidden behind a forgotten archway at Enfield Chambers, Low Pavement.

Her ambitious idea of turning the tired looking premises into an old-fashioned tea room was born.

Thea Caffea is not the usual bijoux tea shop affair, but a majestic emporium offering oodles of space to accommodate an army of devoted tea quaffers.

With its chequerboard floor, pretty floral wallpaper and brightly coloured china cups and saucers – all delightfully mismatched and all largely donated by friends and family – this gem has already won a clutch of awards. It was one of the top ten independent businesses in Nottingham in 2014, while

Carolyn herself was named Inspirational Woman of the Year at the 2013 Women in Business Awards.

There are 22 varieties of delicious loose leaf tea to choose from with not a tea bag in sight – your beverage will be brought to you with a large decorative teapot and strainer ensuring you pour the most delicious brew possible.

An accompanying menu of English classics such as cinnamon toast, scones, Lincolnshire plum bread, quiches, farmhouse platters, savoury tarts and freshly made sandwiches are on offer.

The fabulous cake menu changes each day, with favourites such as Bakewell tart, Eccles cakes and Victoria sponges (no American style brownies or muffins here).

Open for morning, lunch and afternoon tea, everything is served to you at your table – and staff are happy to help with all your important tea etiquette queries. The vintage and cream tea options in particular are a genuine delight.

Come on Nottingham, who's mashing?

Thea Caffea's
ETON MESS CAKE

This tasty take on the popular English treat was devised by Thea Caffea cook Candy and serves between ten-twelve people.

Ingredients

For the cake

300g self raising flour

300g caster sugar

300g butter

3 eggs

Pink food colouring

Strawberry essence

For the topping

2 tubs mascarpone cheese

Icing sugar to taste

Selection of strawberries and meringues

4 tablespoons strawberry coulis

Method

Heat the oven to 160°c.

Beat together the caster sugar and butter until light and fluffy. Gradually add the eggs and add a spoonful of flour with the last one.

Fold in the remaining flour.

Take half the mixture and dot spoonfuls around a 23cm spring form cake tin, lined with baking paper.

Into the other half of the mixture, add the food colouring and strawberry essence.

Add this to the cake tin and take a skewer, swirling it through the mixture.

Bake for 50-60 minutes until springy to the touch.

Cool for 10 minutes, remove from the tin and then allow to cool completely.

Mix the mascarpone with the icing sugar and strawberry coulis and spread on top of the cake.

Scatter strawberries and meringues on top.

Any time is TIFFIN TIME

Tiffin Tea House is the perfect marriage of concept and location –
celebrating the uniquely British tradition of afternoon tea in a bright
and cheery parlour in West Bridgford.

Walking through the door of Tiffin Tea House is like taking a step back in time – with its adorably old fashioned lace tablecloths, brightly coloured walls and bunting, and hits from the 1940s and 1950s playing gently in the background.

No wonder West Bridgford has completely embraced this magical escape from the 21st century, which was opened by former work pals Diane Elliott and Jo Bounds in 2011.

They'd both spent long hours dreaming of starting their own business, but it was ironically Jo's trip to New Zealand – where café culture has taken on a life of its own – which finally inspired them to go for it.

After finding the ideal premises in the shape of a former dress hire business, Jo and Diane spent three months refurbishing the building to create the extraordinarily pretty room we see today.

There are around 30 delicious teas from around the world to choose from, served from a decorative teapot into delicate china cups. Jo and Diane even create their own handmade tea bags from the loose leaf tea to save you the bother of using a strainer.

Popular with all ages, the counter is packed with delicious homemade fare – including splendidly presented cakes like Victoria sandwich, coffee and walnut, lemon layer, carrot, Battenburg and butterscotch. Chief baker Diane gets through some 40 dozen eggs a week to create these mini masterpieces.

Breakfast is available all day and there's a selection of light lunches, featuring sandwiches, omelettes, salads and the legendary Welsh Rarebit. Make sure you try Afternoon Tea, charmingly served with sandwiches, cakes, scones and even, if you fancy it, a mini bottle of sparkling wine.

A team of 13 now runs the tea room, which is open seven days a week. Tiffin Tea House is also a keen supporter of the Totally Locally initiative, and is committed to using local suppliers and traders whenever possible.

Kuchipudi
Masala Chai

Tiffin Tea House
BUTTERSCOTCH CAKE

A shamelessly indulgent treat based on a classic British favourite. Serves ten.

Ingredients

For the cake

250g margarine

100g caster sugar

150g soft brown sugar

5 eggs, beaten

250g self raising flour, sieved

For the butterscotch filling

85g butter

50g soft brown sugar

50g golden syrup

350g icing sugar

2 tablespoons milk

For the caramel topping

25g butter

25g soft brown sugar

25g golden syrup

2 tablespoons double cream

50g vanilla fudge pieces

Method

For the cake

Heat the oven to 180ºc.

Line two 20cm sandwich tins.

Cream the margarine and sugars together until light in texture and colour.

Gradually beat in the eggs.

Fold in the flour by hand.

Transfer mixture to sandwich tins and bake for 20-25 minutes.

For the butterscotch filling

Melt butter, sugar and syrup until dissolved.

Beat in the icing sugar and add enough milk to achieve spreading consistency.

Leave to cool slightly.

Slice horizontally through the sponges so you have four layers.

Sandwich the layers together with the filling.

For the caramel topping

Melt all the ingredients over a low heat and allow to bubble for 30 seconds.

Leave to cool completely.

Spoon over the layered sponges.

Decorate as desired with vanilla fudge – homemade or otherwise!

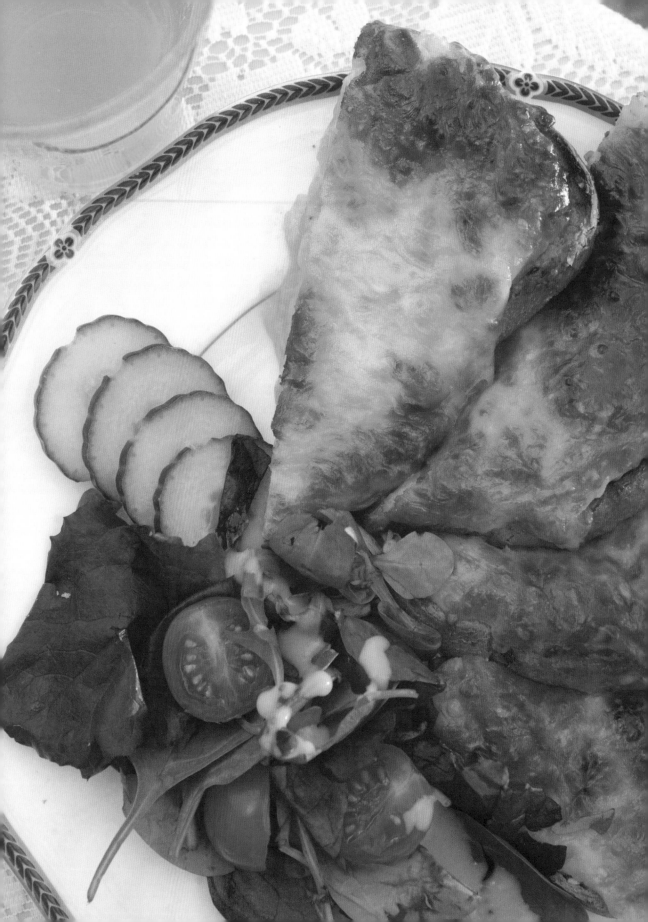

Tiffin's very own
WELSH RAREBIT

Its reputation has grown far and wide in Notts and now the secret to this delicious dish is finally revealed. Serves one-two people.

Ingredients

2 slices of thickly sliced bread

1 egg

2 tablespoons double cream

1 teaspoon English mustard

100-125g grated mature Cheddar cheese

Method

Lightly beat the egg, cream and mustard together.

Stir in the cheese.

Toast bread on both sides.

Divide the cheese mixture evenly onto the toasted bread and place under a hot grill.

Cook until golden and firm to the touch.

Serve piping hot with a salad garnish.

Back to SCHOOL

Tom Brown's Brasserie in Gunthorpe has been teaching Nottinghamshire folk valuable lessons on great food and service for the past 25 years.

Set in an atmospheric old Victorian schoolhouse, Tom Browns Brasserie is one of Nottinghamshire's finest rural restaurants, located in one of the most beautiful parts of the county.

Named in honour of the famous 1857 novel Tom Brown's School Days, written by Thomas Hughes, the charming Gunthorpe building has been elegantly converted to retain its unique history while offering a fresh and contemporary dining experience.

It's a concept that has been put together by the team behind the equally lovely gastropubs the Farndon Boathouse and The Riverbank.

Focusing on top quality modern world cuisine, there are stunning views over the Trent from the outside dining terrace, where you can relax and unwind on lazy summer days or snuggle up next to the outdoor fire pits in winter. They even provide blankets!

This popular restaurant has continuously won critical acclaim and has been featured in the AA Restaurant Guide as well as winning two prestigious AA rosettes recognising the exceptional standard of its food.

As of this year, acclaimed head chef Andrew Brookes has taken control of the menu following extensive experience at several illustrious venues including Cockliffe Country House Hotel, Tonic and the New Ellington in Leeds.

His food ethos is very well suited to the Tom Browns remit – fresh, modern, quirky and fun.

Andrew is looking forward to developing the award winning kitchen here and focusing on maintaining the great quality and brilliant value.

The extensive à la carte menu is packed with gorgeous seasonal fare from succulent steaks and seafood to pork pavé and game. Meanwhile, the versatile Early Bird menu is always a winner, along with the hearty Sunday dinner.

Let's face it, even that villainous bully Flashman would be won over by Tom Brown these days.

Tom Brown's Amalfi Lemon Cheesecake, CASSIS SORBET, VANILLA MERINGUE AND BLACK BERRIES

Another stunning dessert that tastes as good as it looks. Serves six.

Ingredients

For the lemon cheesecake

300g mascarpone cheese

120g caster sugar

3 eggs

5 leaves soaked gelatine

300g lightly whipped cream

100g lemon juice

For the lemon jelly

250g lemon juice

75g sugar

1 vanilla pod

3 soaked gelatine leaves

For the cassis sorbet

500g cassis purée

200g stock syrup

For the Italian meringue

350g caster sugar

100g water

150g egg whites

1 vanilla pods

For the lemon crumble

100g butter

100g caster sugar

1 egg

150g plain flour

Zest of 1 lemon

For the blackcurrant gel

500g blackcurrant purée

5g agar agar

1g xanthan gum

For the meringue shards

100g egg whites

100g icing sugar

100g caster sugar

5g cornflour

Method

For the lemon cheesecake

Whip the eggs and 60g of sugar until fluffy.

Cream the rest of the sugar with the mascarpone.

Warm the lemon juice and add the gelatine. Add to the Mascarpone.

Fold in the egg mixture, then fold in the cream and set.

For the lemon jelly

Warm the lemon juice with the sugar and vanilla pod, add the gelatine and set.

Once set, cut into long strips.

For the cassis sorbet

Mix all the ingredients together and churn in an ice cream machine.

For the Italian meringue

Boil the sugar and water until temperature reaches 121°c.

Whip the egg whites in a machine until just under soft peak.

Turn the machine down to medium speed and slowly add the sugar.

Add the vanilla pod.

For the lemon crumble

Cream the butter and sugar, then add the egg.

Add the flour and lemon zest.

Once a dough is formed, set in the freezer.

Once dough is frozen, finely grate onto a baking mat and bake in the oven at 120°c for 45 minutes.

For the blackcurrant gel

Boil the purée and agar agar, simmer for 4-5 minutes.

Add the gum and set in the fridge.

Once set, cut into chunks and blitz until very smooth.

Pass and set.

For the meringue shards

Whip the egg whites until you have soft peaks. Slowly add the caster sugar.

Fold in the icing sugar and cornflour.

Spread the mixture onto a baking mat until very thin. Sprinkle with some finely chopped freeze-dried blackcurrants.

Put in the oven on its lowest setting until meringue is completely dry.

A proper pub with
PROPER FOOD

The Victoria Hotel in Beeston is that rarest of establishments –
a proper real ale pub which also serves up simply amazing food.

Don't try calling the Victoria Hotel a restaurant or, dare we say it, a "gastro pub" in front of proud owner Neil Kelso.

This is first and foremost a good, old-fashioned pub serving an unparalleled range of cask ales, fine wines and rare malt whiskies which attract a fan base stretching the length of Britain.

But now you mention it, yes, the historic venue also has a cult following amongst foodies thanks to Neil and his team's passion for cooking – inspired by his time spent travelling the world tasting the best cuisine on offer.

He's been at the Freehouse for 20 years now having previously worked as a director for Tynemill Ltd, later the Castle Rock group. Under Neil's reign, the previously run-down boozer has become a local legend, with an enormous extended kitchen offering an ever-changing menu.

Each dish is famously written down on blackboards hung on the wall at the Victoria and you'll never see exactly the same menu line-up twice. An impressive 50% of the options are veggie and there are also brilliant gluten-free choices too.

Choose from sensational dishes such as paella verduras or confit duck, or how about crab, lemon and fresh spinach linguine or chargrilled swordfish.

The extensive seafood choice is highly unusual in a pub – indeed many top restaurants would be unable to match Neil's prowess. Wife Linda takes care of the delicious pudding selection.

Not only have they managed to create a welcoming environment oozing history and character, the 19th century built hotel is a big part of the community here – with regular events such as fish and seafood evenings, wine tastings and an entire charity food, drink and music festival every summer.

Cheers all!

The Victoria's
LINGUINE AI FRUTTI DI MARE

A real favourite at the Vic. Neil has used various combinations of seafood for this dish, depending on availability. Use only the freshest possible. Serves two.

Ingredients

250g good quality dried linguine

50ml dry white wine

60ml olive oil

Knob of butter

2 plump garlic cloves, finely sliced

Good pinch of dried chilli flakes

6 cherry tomatoes, halved

2 small squid, cleaned and thinly sliced into rings, tentacles separated

12 Palourde or Venus clams

12 mussels, scrubbed and de-bearded

8 king prawns, peeled and de-veined

4 large fresh crevettes

2 tablespoon chopped flat-leaf parsley

Salt and freshly ground black pepper

Method

Bring a large pan of well-salted water to a rolling boil.

Clean the crevettes by inserting scissors behind the head and cutting the shell down the back to the tail. Remove any dark intestinal tract, but leave shell on.

In a large sauté pan, slowly heat the olive oil, butter, garlic, tomatoes and chilli flakes until just sizzling. Add the white wine and simmer for 1-2 minutes.

Add the squid rings, tentacles, prawns, crevettes, clams and mussels. Cover with a tight-fitting lid. Turn up the heat and cook for 4-5 minutes, shaking the pan occasionally, until all molluscs are open and seafood cooked through.

Meanwhile, add linguine to boiling water and cook until al dente. Drain and add to sauté pan. Season with salt and pepper, add the parsley and toss well.

Serve with rustic bread or fresh-baked baguette. Supply finger bowls and paper napkins at the side.

This is fantastic with Picpoul de Pinet, Riesling or a pint of Castle Rock Harvest Pale Ale.

Classical ELEGANCE

Step back in time to a more elegant era inside the Walton Hotel in the exclusive Park Estate.

Built in the early 1800s, the Walton Hotel oozes old-style grandeur and glamour with its palatial frontage and lovely outdoor terraced dining area.

It's one of the earliest buildings of The Park Estate, the city's most exclusive neighbourhood which stands on the former deer park of Nottingham Castle.

Originally a hunting lodge, it's now a splendid 15 bedroom hotel with a stylish restaurant focussing on British classics with a modern twist.

Head chef Lee Coates has been at the venue for some two years and has created an engaging menu of familiar dishes including delicious steaks, seafood, Derbyshire lamb and classy vegetarian options – adding his own creative touches to ensure the food here really stands out.

He's keen to evoke a very casual dining experience, with nothing too fussy or stuffy. And yet the quality is never compromised – with many ingredients grown on site and an emphasis on seasonal, locally sourced produce.

The hotel also provides private dining throughout the year, while customers can enjoy great breakfasts, brunches and an extensive bar meal menu during the day.

Expect even more from The Walton in 2015 as the restaurant is completely refurbished in a major project which will recreate the refined ambience of an old shooting lodge, in keeping with the building's fascinating history.

Who needs Downton Abbey when you can have the real thing here?

Jilly Pearson's
LEEK AND STILTON DIP

The Walton Hotel's first recipe is a guest contribution from Jilly Pearson, chair of Nottingham Oasis Breast Cancer Trust. The recipe was originally used in the charity book 'Let's Get Saucy'. Serves four-six as a starter.

Ingredients

A little oil and a knob of butter

2 medium leeks, finely sliced

¼ teaspoon dried chilli

½ glass of white wine

1 tablespoon chopped tarragon

1 clove of garlic, crushed and finely chopped

200g cream cheese

90g Stilton cheese, crumbled

30g walnuts, roughly broken

Method

Preheat oven to 180°c.

Heat the oil and butter in a pan.

Add the leeks, chilli and a good glug of wine.

Sauté the leeks until the wine has been absorbed. Add the garlic and tarragon and cook for one minute.

In a bowl, mix the leeks with the cream cheese and Stilton.

Transfer the mixture to a small ovenproof dish. Sprinkle the walnuts over the top.

Bake for 25-30 minutes until the dip is bubbling.

To serve, spoon onto chicory or Little Gem lettuce leaves. Great with celery or warm, toasted ciabbata.

Anne Davies'
PEA AND CHORIZO RISOTTO

The Walton's second recipe is contributed by BBC East Midlands Today presenter Anne Davies, who says this is one of her family's staple dishes, created when her sons were schoolboys – they're now in their 20s and love it just as much. She adores cooking and coming up with new ideas, but says her risotto is her favourite. Perfect as a starter or as a warming hearty meal on a cold winter's evening. Serves four.

Ingredients

25g butter

Splash of olive oil

1 red onion, chopped

Half a chorizo sausage, chopped into small pieces

250g arborio rice

1 large glass of good quality white wine

1 litre chicken stock

100g frozen petit pois

Handful Parmesan cheese, grated

Black pepper and sea salt to taste

Method

In a large pan, melt the butter with a splash of oil. Sauté the onion until softened.

Add the chorizo and fry for two minutes to release the spicy orange oils.

Throw in the rice and stir until coated in oil. Cook until the oil has disappeared.

Add the wine and follow with one ladle of stock, stirring constantly until the liquid is absorbed.

Continue adding one ladle of stock at a time for around 15 minutes, allowing all the liquid to be absorbed before adding the next ladle (you may not need all the stock, equally you may need to top up with a drop of water if the stock runs out – it varies depending on the absorption of the rice).

When the rice is cooked, add the petit pois and heat through. Finish with a handful of Parmesan and combine.

Sprinkle extra Parmesan on the top and serve with a lightly dressed green salad.

The Walton Hotel's
ELDERFLOWER POSSET

This is chef Lee Coates' own dessert dish – a refreshing palate cleanser ideal for lazy summer days. Serves two.

Ingredients

750ml double cream

225g caster sugar

1 teaspoon lemon juice

75ml elderflower cordial

Method

In a pan, boil the cream and sugar together, ensuring the sugar is fully dissolved.

Simmer for two minutes until reduced, then add the lemon juice and elderflower cordial.

Transfer to a glass bowl or mould and allow to set in the fridge, ideally overnight.

Serve with fresh berries or a fruit coulis, and shortbread biscuits.

Made at WELBECK

The Welbeck Estate in north Notts plays host to two of the region's most prestigious businesses – The School of Artisan Food and the Welbeck Farm Shop.

It's one of the great traditional landed estates and now Welbeck, in the heart of Sherwood Forest, is equally renowned for its thriving sustainable businesses, with a strong emphasis on food.

The School of Artisan Food has an international reputation for its superb courses, ranging from day sessions to a year-long diploma in artisan food production – the first of its kind in the UK.

Staffed and run by experts whose skills are matched only by their passion, students here enjoy a truly unrivalled learning experience, with people of all skill levels expanding their knowledge of food techniques.

The School is housed in the former fire stables, dating back to 1870, with state-of-the-art refurbished training rooms specially equipped for teaching baking and patisserie, cheesemaking, butchery and charcuterie, brewing, preserving plus ice cream and chocolate making.

Close by, the Welbeck Farm Shop is packed with mouthwatering produce from Nottinghamshire, South

Yorkshire, Lincolnshire and Derbyshire, earning it a local and national reputation.

The shop also features top quality produce from the Welbeck Estate – including Stichelton cheese, Welbeck Bakehouse artisan bread, Welbeck Abbey Brewery real ales and Boutique Aromatique chocolates, patisserie and confectionery.

The award-winning butchery team apply their fine craftsmanship to all the counter's produce – whether it's Welbeck's own seasonal game and venison, lamb reared on the estate, or cured meats made using their own time-honoured recipes in the specialist maturing room.

Meanwhile, on the cheese and deli counter, the resident cheese and dairy expert works closely with Neal's Yard Dairy to give customers exciting and diverse cheeses, as well as taking care of the specialist ageing room.

In-house, this amazing shop produces a wide array of deli items, including cold cuts, meat and vegetarian pastries, fresh salads and sausage rolls. There are also seasonal fruits and vegetables from a trusted network of local growers.

The Welbeck Estate

Welbeck Ale and Beef
COBBLER WITH STICHELTON SCONES

A stunning winter dish from the experts at The School of Artisan Food using fabulous ingredients available at the Welbeck Farm Shop. Serves six-eight.

Ingredients

For the stew

Vegetable oil, for frying

3 tablespoons plain flour

Salt and freshly ground black pepper

900g chuck/stewing steak, cubed

2 onions, sliced

2 carrots, cut into chunks

2 sticks celery, cut into 2cm pieces

1 bottle Portland Black Welbeck Abbey Brewery beer

600ml beef stock

1 bay leaf and a few sprigs of thyme

For the scone topping

225g self raising flour

50g butter

140ml milk

Pinch salt

150g Stichelton cheese

Milk or beaten egg

Method

Preheat oven to 180°c.

Toss the beef in seasoned flour until well coated.

Heat half the oil in a flameproof casserole dish on the hob and brown meat in batches.

Set browned beef aside, heat the remaining oil in the same pan and fry the onions, carrots and celery until just coloured.

Remove from the heat and pour the Portland Black into the casserole and, whilst heating, use a wooden spoon or spatula to loosen any meat or vegetables from the dish.

Return the meat to the casserole with the stock and herbs, cover and cook in oven for approximately 1½ hours, or until the meat is tender.

Meanwhile make the scone topping. Put the flour and salt into a bowl and then rub in the butter until mix looks like fine breadcrumbs. Crumble in 100g of the cheese and mix together.

Add sufficient milk to bring dough together. You may not need all the milk and you should take care not to overwork the dough.

Tip out onto floured surface, press together gently and shape to about 2.5cm thick. Cut out circles of dough.

Brush top of each scone with beaten egg or milk and sprinkle on remaining Stichelton.

Remove stew from oven and place scones on top, increase oven temperature to 220°c and return stew uncovered for a further 25-30 minutes until scones are golden.

Service
WITH STYLE

World Service is Nottingham's premier fine dining restaurant and lounge bar, winning critical acclaim both locally and nationally.

Established in 2000, World Service offers an effortlessly stylish fine dining experience which has been run to great success by the same management team since day one.

Their vision was to create an old-fashioned colonial feel inside the elegant surroundings of the 17th century Newdigate House, a building most recently used as the home of the Nottingham and Notts United Services Club.

The beautiful, individually made furniture and richly ornamental décor imagines a gentleman traveller who has seen the world and brought home a feast of treasures to create a fascinating east meets west style.

And this subtly adventurous theme continues with the food, which provides a fabulous fusion of tastes and influences from around the world.

The lunch and à la carte menu change frequently, with chefs bringing their own unique interpretation to dishes.

The French connection is very much en vogue in 2014, with Valentin Petiteau creating main courses such as fillet of beef, dauphinoise potatoes, roasted carrot purée, and buttered kale.

The local influence is also important, as demonstrated by options such as Nottinghamshire baked beetroot, with honey roast chicory, caramelised onion purée, crispy walnut loaf and Bosworth Ash goats cheese.

The beautiful gardens in this busy city centre location provide a secret and unexpected pleasure, while the private rooms offer a formal and impressive dining option in the grand traditions of a richly historic building.

It's no surprise that you can find World Service in the AA, Good Food and Michelin guides, or that the venue took top spot at the Nottingham Restaurant of the Year awards for four out of the seven years they ran.

Meanwhile, the extensive wine list – offering a choice of around 300 finest vintages – reflect the high standards of food and service at this refined and much-loved Nottingham institution.

World Service's
POACHED WILD TURBOT WITH
OYSTER MAYONNAISE, FENNEL AND DASHI

This exquisite dish is brilliant served with mashed potato and crispy seaweed.
Serves four.

Ingredients

4 portions of wild turbot
(approximately 180g per portion)

1 bay leaf

2 large carrots

1 fennel bulb

1 shallot

1 baking potato

200g parsley

3 oysters

2 egg yolks

½ lemon, juiced

2½ litres water

30g kombu seaweed

15g bonito flakes

300ml rapeseed oil

Sea salt

Muslin cloth

Method

For the oyster mayonnaise

Blanch and chop parsley.

Add to blender and cover with the rapeseed oil. Blend for two minutes.

Place in muslin cloth and leave to drain into a container overnight.

Open oysters the next day and mix in a blender with the egg yolks, lemon juice, and pinch of sea salt.

Combine with parsley oil then pass through a fine sieve.

Keep cool in fridge until ready to use.

For the rest of the dish

Chop one carrot, the potato and the centre of the fennel into small cubes and blanch in boiling water for three minutes.

When cooked, drain and keep in the fridge.

In a pan bring half a litre of water to 85ºc, and then add the kombu seaweed.

Leave to infuse for 20 minutes.

Remove the kombu and repeat the process in the same water with the bonito flakes.

Pass through muslin cloth and reserve the infused liquid (known as "dashi").

In another pan bring the remaining two litres of water to the boil.

Add one roughly chopped carrot, fennel offcuts, one chopped shallot, bay leaf and a pinch of salt.

Add the turbot and leave to simmer for eight minutes.

Whilst the turbot is cooking, reheat the diced vegetables in a small pan with a splash of the dashi and oyster mayonnaise.

Serve the turbot on a bed of the diced vegetables.

Pour a small amount of dashi over the fish, and a few dots of the oyster mayonnaise around the edge of the plate.

Yossi Eliyahoo's
THAI BEEF SALAD

Following several restaurant successes in Tel Aviv, restaurant entrepreneur Yossi Eliyahoo arrived in Nottingham in 2002 to create the concept restaurant, Chino Latino.

Yossi has since gone on to work with some of the world's top chefs to create unique restaurant experiences in capital cities such as Amsterdam, Berlin and Barcelona. He even scooped the head chef of Nobu London for his restaurants in Amsterdam, MoMo, Izakaya and speakeasy bar and kitchen The Butcher, which attract the likes of Rihanna and Robin van Persie.

Despite all the international glamour however, Nottingham remains Yossi's home. "Nottingham is where my family and I are based and where I relax between hectic travelling schedules. The city has a special place in my heart. It's where my international career started off and my family has grown. It also has an excellent choice of restaurants including my favourites Iberico and MemSaab. And who knows, should the right opportunity arise, I may even open something here again soon!"

Serves two-four.

Ingredients

For the salad

6 medium tomatoes

1 large cucumber

1 bunch fresh mint

1 bunch fresh coriander

½ red onion

2 garlic cloves

2-3 bird's-eye chillies, to taste

Juice of 1 lemon

4 tablespoons Thai fish sauce

For the beef

2 sirloin steaks (approximately 275g each)

Olive oil

Black pepper

(All ingredients should be at room temperature before preparation)

Method

For the salad

Slice the tomatoes into 8 parts each.

Dice the cucumber by chopping off the ends, slicing down the middle lengthways, scooping out the middle seeds and chopping into small sections.

Chop the red onion into very thin slices.

Crush the garlic cloves.

Chop the bird's-eye chillies into fine slices, keeping the seeds.

Tear the leaves off all the mint and coriander stalks, discard the stalks.

Add all of the above ingredients into a large salad bowl, pour over the juice of the lemon and the Thai fish sauce, mix and put aside to let the flavours infuse.

For the beef

Massage the beef with cooking olive oil both sides and season the upside with lots of crushed black pepper – don't be shy with the pepper, it's very important for the flavour and it's never too much!

Heat a heavy duty, thick-based frying pan to a high heat, until it is smoking.

Add the steak into the pan with pepper side down, season the other side with black pepper.

Cook for approximately 2½ minutes each side – the steak needs to be seared on the outside and juicy on the inside (medium/rare).

Take the steak out of the pan, let it rest for a few seconds, cut the fat off the edge and slice the meat into thin slices.

Add the sliced beef and the juices from the chopping board into the salad and mix together – doing this straight away will allow the flavours from the steak juices and citrus to infuse together and will stop the steak from cooking further. Let it rest for a few minutes.

To serve

Serve on its own or with a bowl of long grain basmati rice.

All of our food is made
fresh to order
At busy times, your
served with
chunky toast
£3.95
toasted
banana +
walnut loaf
£2.95
served with
butter
Billionaire's
Shortbread
£1.95
£2.95
served with
butter
delilah

for 2 to share £12.95

Rocky
Road
£1.95

Choccy
Crispy
Chew
£1.95

Biscotti
Italia

The DIRECTORY

These great businesses have supported the making of this book; please support and enjoy them.

200 Degrees Coffee
Heston House, Meadow Lane,
Nottingham NG2 3HE
Telephone: 07733 446503
Website: www.200degs.com
Artisan coffee roasters, sourcing all of their green coffee beans from Rainforest Alliance certified farms.

Annie's Burger Shack
5 Broadway, Lace Market,
Nottingham NG1 1PR
Email: bookingatannies@gmail.com
Website: www.anniesburgershack.com
Real ale and handcrafted authentic American burgers, made to order with a range of exciting seasoning and toppings.

Asiana
Dabell Avenue, Blenheim Industrial
Estate, Nottingham NG6 8WA
Telephone: 0115 977 1888
Website: www.asianaltd.com
A family run business importing ingredients and homeware from countries in the far east, and distributing nationally to restaurants, takeaways and supermarkets.

Aubrey's Traditional Creperie
14-16, West End Arcade, Long Row,
Nottingham NG1 6JP
Telephone: 0115 947 0855
Website: www.aubreystraditional
creperie.com
Traditional Breton galettes and crêpes combined with fresh ingredients and toppings, one of which is Aubrey's homemade salted caramel.

Blue Monkey Brewery
10 Pentrich Rd, Giltbrook Industrial
Park, Nottingham NG16 2UZ
The Organ Grinder, 21 Alfreton Road,
Nottingham NG7 3JE
The Organ Grinder, 4 Wood Gate,
Loughborough, Leicestershire LE11
2TY
The Organ Grinder, 21 Portland St,
Newark NG24 4XF
Telephone: 0115 938 5899
Website: www.bluemonkey
brewery.com
An award-winning brewery with several pubs called The Organ Grinder in Nottingham, Loughborough and Newark.

Brown Betty's
17B St James's St,
Nottingham NG1 6FH
Telephone: 0115 941 3464
Website: www.brownbettys.co.uk
Sandwich and deli shop in the heart of the city, serving breakfast, ciabattas, salads. sloppy Joes and more.

The Cheese Shop
6 Flying Horse Walk,
Nottingham NG1 2HN
Telephone: 0115 941 9114
Website: www.cheeseshop-
nottingham.co.uk
Family run delicatessen selling over 200 British cheeses and continental cheese from all over Europe.

Clock House Café
Upton Hall, Main Street, Upton,
Nottinghamshire NG23 5TE
Telephone: 01636 919591
Website: www.clockhousecafé.co.uk
Café and tea room specialising in breakfasts, brunch, home cooked lunch and full afternoon tea with a delicious cakes, scones and sweet treats.

The Cod's Scallops
170 Bramcote Lane, Wollaton,
Nottingham NG8 2QP
Telephone: 0115 985 4107
Website: www.codsscallops.com
Restaurant, fishmongers and takeaway serving classic fish and chips cooked in real beef dripping and deep fried in secret recipe batter. The freshest daily catch from the coastlines of the UK as well as homemade pies and award winning sausages.

Colwick Cheese – Belvoir Vale Creamery
Crossroads Farm, Scalford Rd, Melton Mowbray, Leicestershire LE14 4EF
Telephone: 01949 860242
Website: www.belvoirridgecreamery. wordpress.com
Not commercially made for years, Belvoir Vale Creamery specialise in soft Colwick cheese made from the milk of their award-winning Red Poll & Blue Albion cattle.

Delilah Fine Foods
12 Victoria St, Nottingham NG1 2EX
Telephone: 0115 948 4461
Website: www.delilahfinefoods.co.uk
Independent delicatessen and fine food and wine merchant, offering breakfast, brunch and culinary treats.

Edin's Deli Café
15 Broad St, Nottingham NG1 3AJ
Telephone: 0115 924 1112
Website: www.edinsnottingham.co.uk
Vibrant continental café bar serving home cooked food, made from local produce.
Edin's Kitchen
15 Carlton Street, Hockley,
Nottingham NG1 1NL
Telephone: 0115 950 1172
Website: www.edinsnottingham.co.uk
Tasty and healthy food made with fresh market produce. Also serving freshly ground coffee and homemade cakes pies, tarts and petit fours.

escabeche
25-27 Bridgford Rd, West Bridgford,
Nottingham, NG2 6AU
Telephone: 0115 981 7010
Website: www.escabeche.co.uk
A taste of the mediterranean with freshly cooked tapas, raciones, breakfast, drinks and desserts.

Experience Nottinghamshire
1-3 Smithy Row,
Nottingham NG1 2BY
Telephone: 0844 477 5678
Website: www.experiencenotting hamshire.com
Official tourism body for Nottinghamshire.

Farndon Boathouse
The Riverside, Newark-on-Trent,
Nottinghamshire NG24 3SX
Telephone: 01636 676578
Website: www.farndonboathouse.co.uk
Bar and restaurant situated on the leafy banks of the River Trent, serving homemade and locally produced food, including in-house smoked meats and herbs from the garden.

Fire & Ice
40 Bridgford Rd, West Bridgford,
Nottingham NG2 6AP
Telephone: 0115 981 9000
Website: www.fireandicewb.co.uk
Family run bar and restaurant specialising in an impressive range of cocktails and wood fired pizzas.

Fred Hallam Ltd
23 High Rd, Beeston,
Nottingham NG9 2JQ
Telephone: 0115 925 4766
Website: www.fredhallam.com
Established in 1908 supplying fresh fish as well as local and continental fruit and vegetables throughout the community for over 100 years.

Gonalston Farm Shop
Southwell Rd,
Nottingham NG14 7DR
Telephone: 0115 966 5666
Website: www.gonalstonfarmshop. co.uk
Offering only the very freshest of produce to the local community with an emphasis on exquisite taste and variety.

Hart's
Standard Hill, Park Row,
Nottingham NG1 6GN
Telephone: 0115 988 1900
Website: www.hartsnottingham.co.uk
Modern British cooking using top quality locally sourced ingredients in striking combinations.

Homemade
20 Pelham Sreet,
Nottingham NG1 2EG
632 Mansfield Road, Sherwood,
Nottingham NG5 2GA
Forest Recreation Ground Pavilion,
Nottingham NG5 2BU
Telephone: 0115 924 3030 (Hockley)
0115 962 6020 (Sherwood)
0115 978 1608 (Pavilion)
Website: www.homemadecafé.com
Does what it says on the tin. Homemade
fresh food from sandwiches and jacket
potatoes to burgers, cakes and sweet treats.

Iberico
The Shire Hall, High Pavement,
Nottinghamshire NG1 1HN
Telephone: 0115 941 0410
Website: www.ibericotapas.com
World tapas combining the rustic
simplicity of the Spanish cooking with
refined styles across the globe.

J T Beedham Butchers
556 Mansfield Rd,
Nottingham NG5 2FS
Telephone: 0115 960 5901
Website: www.jtbeedham.com
Purveyors of English meat since 1884.
Boasting gold award winning speciality
sausages, traditional home dry cured bacon
and Eastern European dried smoked
meats prepared in Beedham's very own
smoke house.

Kayal
8 Broad St, Nottingham NG1 3AL
Telephone: 0115 941 4733
Website: www.kayalrestaurant.com
Tasty and healthy global food
maintaining tradition, quality, creativity
and fresh ingredients and aromas.

Larder on Goosegate
1st Floor, 16-22 Goosegate, Hockley,
Nottingham NG1 1FE
Telephone: 0115 950 0111
Website: www.thelarderon
goosegate.co.uk
Classic British dishes with a modern twist
using the best seasonal ingredients.

MemSaab
12-14 Maid Marian Way,
Nottingham NG1 6HS
Telephone: 0115 957 0009
Website: www.mem-saab.co.uk
Fining dining Indian restaurant
featuring traditional perfectly spiced
curries through to modern Indian cooking.

The Moleface Pub Company
The Wollaton, Lambourne Drive,
Wollaton, Nottingham NG8 1GR
Telephone: 0115 928 8610
Larwood & Voce, Fox Road, West
Bridgford, Nottingham NG2 6AJ
Telephone: 0115 981 9960
The Lord Nelson, Chestnut Grove,
Burton Joyce, Nottingham NG14 5DN
Telephone: 0115 931 1800
The Royal Oak, Main Road, Radcliffe-
on-Trent, Nottingham NG12 2FD
Tel: 0115 933 5659
Website: www.molefacepubcompany.
co.uk
One of the city's most loved pub groups,
The Moleface Pub Company has four
venues serving up seasonal menus in
relaxed surroundings.

Perkins
Station Rd, Plumtree,
Nottingham NG12 5NA
Telephone: 0115 937 3695
Website: www.perkinsrestaurant.co.uk
Versatile daily menus championing local
produce from the surrounding villages
and regularly featuring dishes from their
very own smokehouse.

Pudding Pantry
27/29 Trinity Square,
Nottingham NG1 4AF
Tel: 0115 950 4660
Website: www.thepuddingpantry.co.uk
Delicious cakes, puddings, desserts baked
in-house, accompanied by artisan coffee.

The Riverbank
Trent Bridge Buildings,
West Bridgford,
Nottingham NG2 5FB
Telephone: 0115 986 7960
Website: www.riverbanknotts.co.uk
Situated near Trent Bridge with its
stunning riverside views it's been
extensively converted into a stylish and
modern 250-capacity bar and 110-seater
restaurant, with a separate gallery
function room and an in-house deli.

Sat Bains With Rooms
Lenton Lane, Nottingham NG7 2SA
Telephone: 0115 986 6566
Website: www.restaurantsatbains.com
Notingham's most famous eatery, Sat
Bains is a two star Michelin restaurant
serving modern British cuisine with eight
bedrooms.

Sauce Shop
117 Gordon Road, West Bridgford
NG2 5LX
Telephone 07956 711166
Website: www.sauce-shop.co.uk
Nottingham based sauce brand with a colourful range of 100% natural savoury and sweet sauces.

Savai
Plumptre House, 5 Poplar St,
Nottingham NG1 1GP
Telephone: 0115 958 6828
Website: www.pizzeriasavai.co.uk
Family run Italian restaurant focusing on fresh, good quality ingredients and homemade food.

School of Artisan Food
Lower Motor Yard, Worksop,
Nottinghamshire S80 3LR
Telephone: 01909 532171
Website: www.schoolofartisanfood.org
Teaching short courses or advanced diplomas in all areas of artisan food production, from breadmaking, cheesemaking, brewing, butchery, charcuterie and preserving.

Shipstones Brewery
Belvoir Brewery, Station Road,
Old Dalby LE14 3NE
Telephone: 0115 8716477
Website: www.shipstones.com
Nottingham brewers since 1852, producing award winning traditional ales.

Sinatra
8-16 Chapel Bar,
Nottingham NG1 6JQ
Telephone: 0115 941 1050
Website: www.sinatrabarandrestaurant.co.uk
European bar and restaurant serving a variety of food from the continent as well as a range of drinks and cocktails.

Thaymar Farm Shop & Ice Cream
Haughton Park Farm, Near
Bothamsall, Retford,
Nottinghamshire DN22 8DB
Telephone: 01623 862632
Website: www.thaymaricecream.co.uk
Family farm with shop and tea room, creating a variety of ice cream flavours using quality local fruit and natural flavours.

Thea Caffea
14a Low Pavement,
Nottingham, NG1 7DG
Telephone: 0115 9412110
Website: www.facebook.com/TheaCaffea
Family owned and run traditional English tearoom serving extensive selection of loose leaf tea alongside a food menu synonymous with tearoom fayre.

Tiffin Tea House
35 Abbey Rd, West Bridgford,
Nottingham, NG2 5NG
Telephone: 0115 981 6224
Website: www.tiffin-teahouse.co.uk
Providing all of the comforts of the great British tradition of afternoon tea, serving fresh food, home baked cakes and a wide selection of speciality teas, coffee and cold drinks. Seasonal food from locally sourced produce.

Tom Brown's
Trentside, Gunthorpe,
Nottingham NG14 7FB
Telephone: 0115 966 3642
Website: www.tombrowns.co.uk
Two AA rosette restaurant combining the stunning charm and character of an old Victorian school house with an elegant, contemporary interior.

The Victoria
85 Dovecote Lane,
Nottingham NG9 1JG
Telephone: 0115 925 4049
Website: www.victoriabeeston.co.uk
Pub and restaurant and hotel dating back to 1840, with an ever changing chalk boarded menu based on market availability.

The Walton Hotel
2 North Road,
Nottingham NG7 1AG
Telephone: 0115 947 5215
Website: www.thewaltonhotel.com
Luxury boutique hotel situated in the historic Park estate in Nottingham. With a lively bar and stylish restaurant serving à la carte, lighter bites and seasonal menus.

The Welbeck Estate
Worksop, Nottinghamshire S80 3LW
Telephone: 01909 478725
Website: www.welbeck.co.uk/experience/visit/farm-shop
Offering produce from Nottinghamshire, South Yorkshire, Lincolnshire and Derbyshire, earning both a local and national reputation selling meat, cheeses and fruit and vegetables.

World Service
Newdigate House, Castle Gate,
Nottingham NG1 6AF
Telephone: 0115 847 5587
Website: www.worldservicerestaurant.com
Uniquely housed in the elegant surroundings of 17th Century Newdigate House, a premier fine dining restaurant and lounge bar blending the customs and traditions of the buildings' past and heritage.